Forms for a public address

Surpllus

FORMS FOR A PUBLIC ADDRESS

Tom Nicholson and Jan Svenungsson,
in conversation

Saturday, 16 February, 2008

JS —— This is where it starts, one morning in Helsinki, far from home—although further from your home than mine. It's a cold and windy day, –7 degrees Celsius, yet there's no snow on the ground.

Yesterday at dusk, we scaled the old ramparts at Suomenlinna, the fortress island 8
guarding the approach to the city. I showed you a small disused sports ground, where in 1918, during Finland's Civil War, the Whites executed Red prisoners. Seventy-four years later, I had an exhibition in the building next to the sports ground which by then had become an arts centre. The most interesting feature of that show was that the distribution of the works had been randomly determined by a computer; a meaningful meaningless gesture, now lost in time.

Before I left for the airport this morning we discussed how this dialogue should work and I proposed using the title of your presentation at the Academy of Fine Arts two days ago as some sort of a theme: 'Forms for a public address'.

I like this title. It sounds both serious and formal but the effect is not off-putting, instead it's rather intriguing.

How do you define the public you aim to address, and will they listen?

TN —— While we were in Helsinki—enjoying all that misty cold weather, those icy

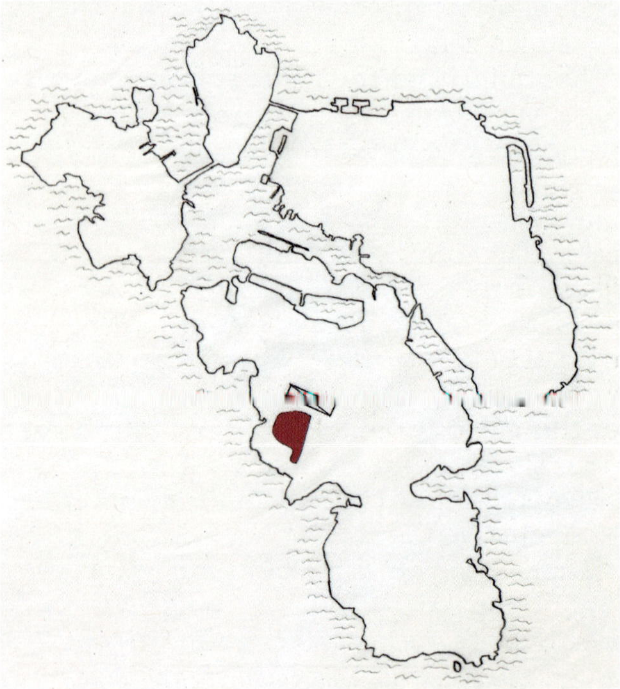

Suomenlinna. Sports ground in red.
Map: Jan Svenungsson.

winds off the water at Suomenlinna—a significant 'public address' took place in Australia. The Prime Minister Kevin Rudd made a formal apology in Parliament to the 'stolen generations', the generations of Aboriginal and Torres Strait Islander children separated from their families and communities by the state under national assimilation policies. Rudd's speech was televised and broadcast live, watched and listened to around the country in public places, including large gatherings of stolen generations survivors outside Parliament itself. It was moving to see the responses of those people who had long been asking for this apology and for whom it held enormous significance. I also felt an ambivalence towards the gesture though, mainly because I thought it was directed at non-Aboriginal Australia; a kind of self-addressed gesture of redemption or absolution, with its glaring refusal of any form of compensation for the stolen generations. The address was carefully choreographed, tightly worded (constant references to 'Australia', 'Australians', 'moving forward', 'a new page'), never threatening to open itself out to the contradictions of the gesture, insistently unifying—the logic of a classical public 'monument', but in a form for the electronic age.

To answer your question about my somewhat smaller set of public actions (!), there

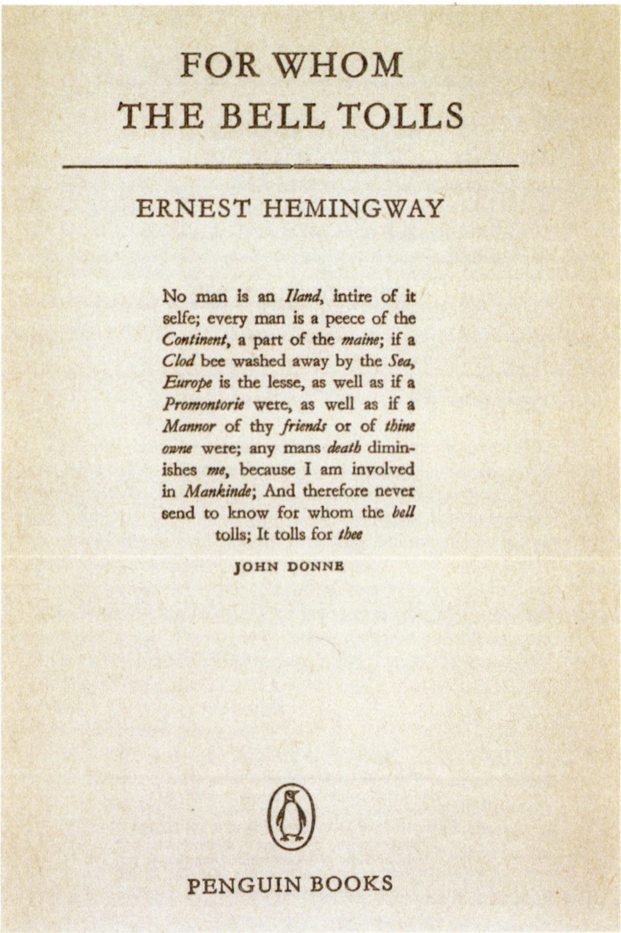

FOR WHOM
THE BELL TOLLS

ERNEST HEMINGWAY

No man is an *Iland*, intire of it selfe; every man is a peece of the *Continent*, a part of the *maine*; if a *Clod* bee washed away by the *Sea*, *Europe* is the lesse, as well as if a *Promontorie* were, as well as if a *Mannor* of thy *friends* or of *thine owne* were; any mans *death* diminishes *me*, because I am involved in *Mankinde*; And therefore never send to know for whom the *bell* tolls; It tolls for *thee*

JOHN DONNE

PENGUIN BOOKS

Tom Nicholson, *After action for another library* (detail). 1999–2001/2006.
Type C photograph, 60 × 90 cm.

Action for another library was established in Melbourne in response to the systematic destruction of books and libraries by the Indonesian military in the aftermath of the UN-sponsored ballot on independence in East Timor in 1999. During the two-year life of the action, thousands of books were donated by bookstores, libraries, and individuals in and around Melbourne. These books were shipped to Dili in containers where they now form part of the nascent National University Library of East Timor.

is an ambiguous attitude towards 'the public'
in those banner marches. They mostly take 14, 16
place at dawn. In a paradoxical way, that proj-
ect functioned in a more public way through
its traces in a gallery space. That paradox is
more pronounced in other works, like *After* 10
action for another library. As a public work,
that action is almost completely invisible.
It is only through the accumulation and
presentation of its residues that it assumes a
'public address'. In some ways, my impulses
are towards the second meaning in our title's
double entendre, that is, public address as a
public site, rather than as a public form of
speech. Partly there is an attraction to the
visual languages and histories which are
only available—as a kind of field into which
the work is inserted—in the public sphere.
But there is also an attraction to chance: the
serendipitous meanings that a work accu-
mulates through the events and forms that
occur alongside it or around it.

JS —— So the 'public' does not consist of 'everyone', but is made up of people who have decided they wish to be addressed by you, the artist. Of course, if your action had been expressly defined as a political act, in the form of a speech, for example, most of the audience would have consisted of people who had received the information that you would talk at a certain place and time, and

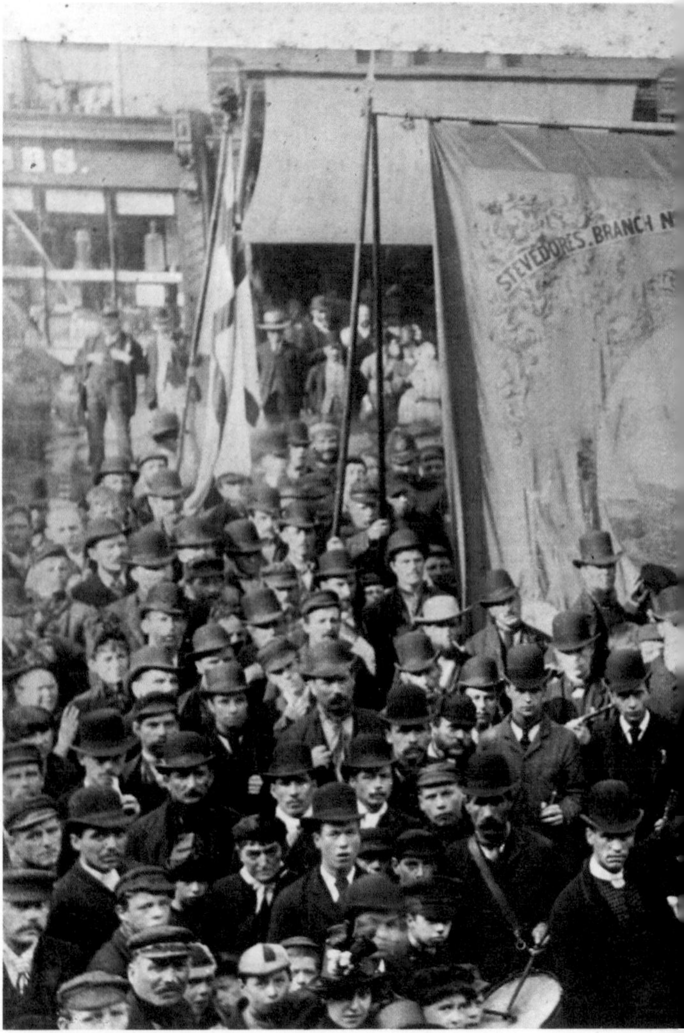

Photographer unknown, *Great dock strike 1889*, 1889, black and white photograph.
By permission of the People's History Museum, Manchester, UK.

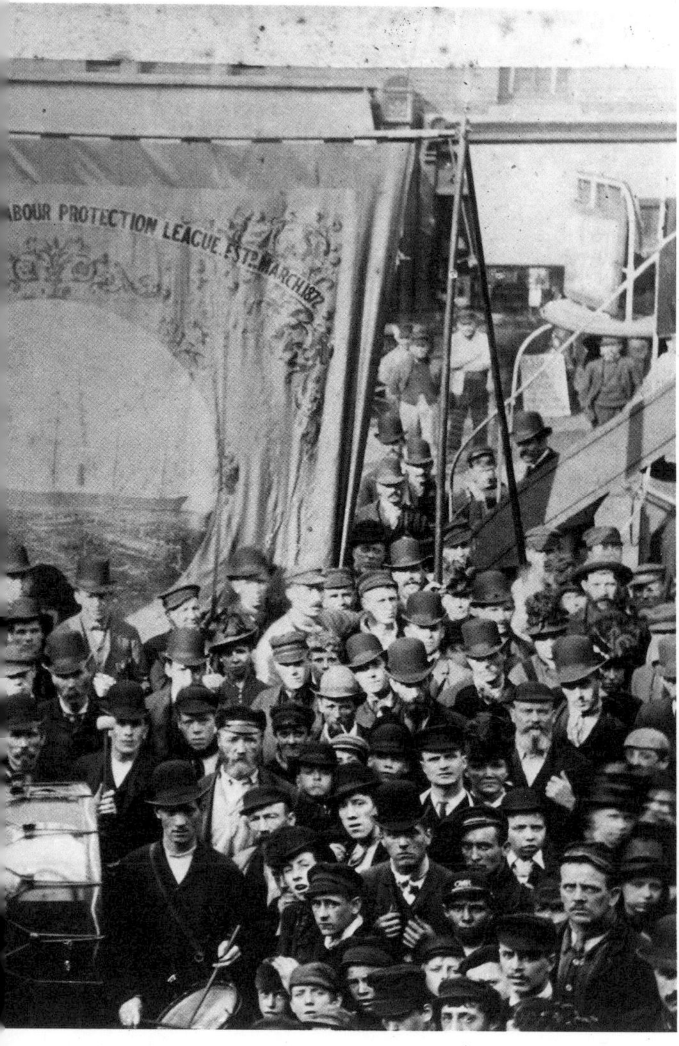
ABOUR PROTECTION LEAGUE. ESTD. MARCH 1872

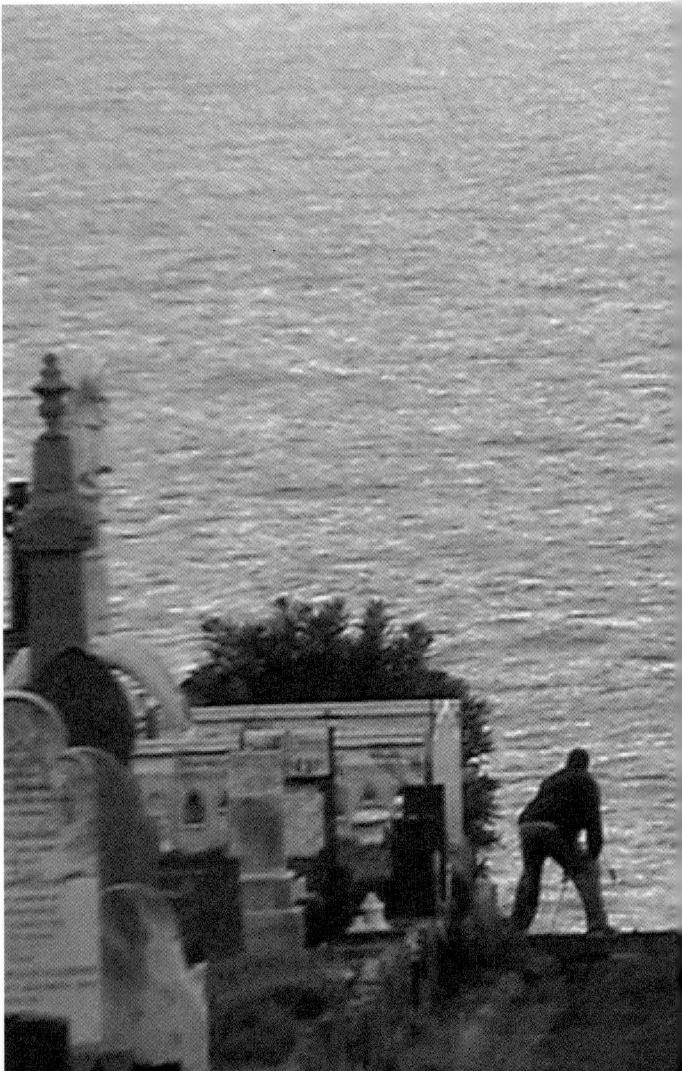

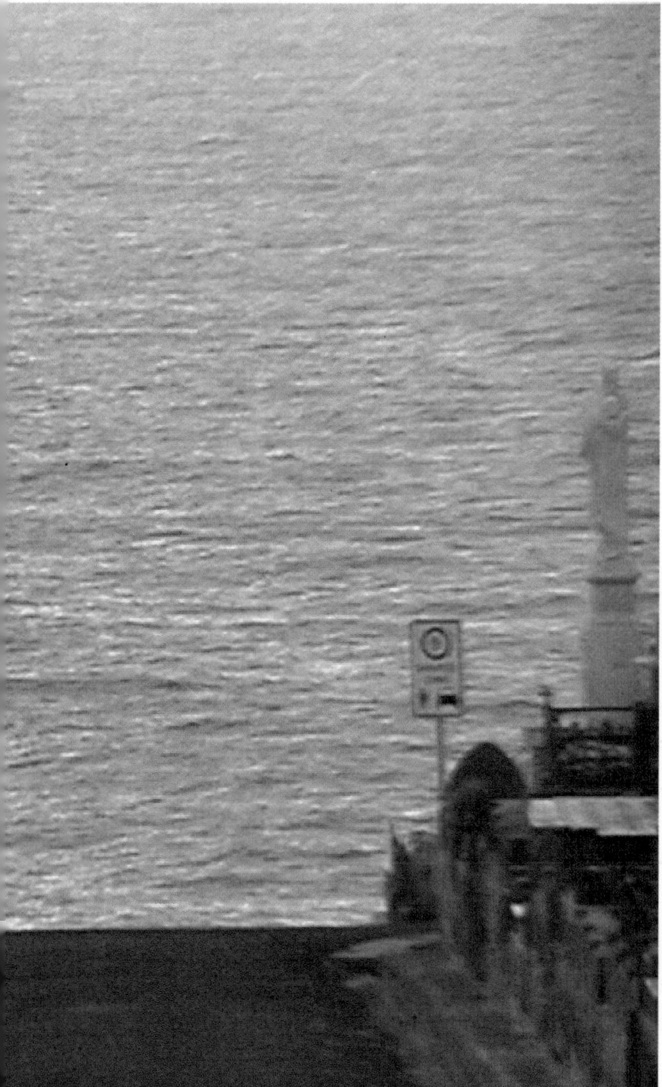

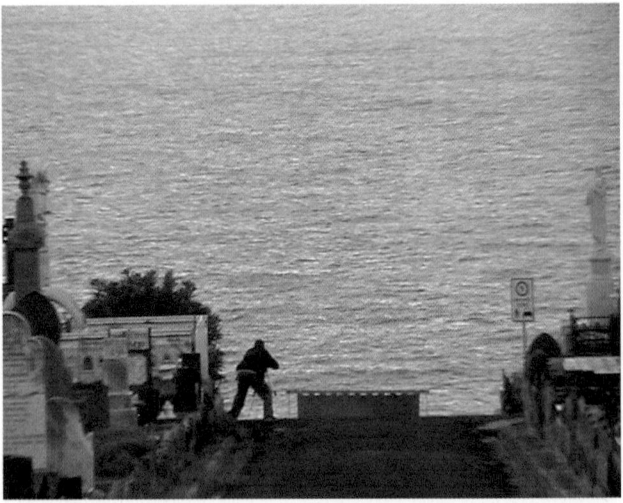

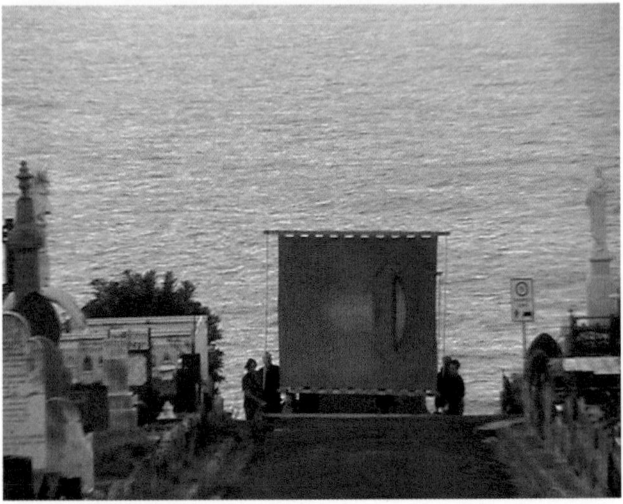

Above and previous spread:
Tom Nicholson, video stills from *Documents from a banner marching project 2004–2007*, 2004–2007, three-channel SD digital video and super 8 film transferred to digital video, duration: 19 mins 9 seconds, held in the collection of the National Gallery of Victoria.

they would have chosen to come. To me, however, one of the factors which make the traces (i.e. the videos) of the banner marches so attractive is that they, in a quiet, respectful and rather unassuming way, seem to introduce an anarchic element in the everyday life of a city. Non-violent anarchic behaviour in public space can be a kind of poetry. At the same time, while I am writing this in April (I know my response is late, but I've been submerged in work both in Sweden and here in Germany) tension is building around the Olympic Torch relay, which has become a very different form of public address. State sponsored, security dependent, nostalgic (1936), nevertheless it is literally running out of control.

TN —— One of the tensions in that banner marching project is between the nature of the banner march and a certain anarchic character. Banner marching is a classically 12
socialist form, precisely because of its reliance upon the cohesion of many bodies, its articulation of many agents into a collective, which is symbolically expressed in the banner through the participants' shared affiliation with the banner's message, but also physically, through the coordination required to carry the object itself. Since the banners I produced for the marches bear no clear message, this cohesion became mis-

placed or stressed, a fact exaggerated by the size of the banners and their awkwardness as objects, which required five or more people to carry in coordination. This awkwardness is persistently evident in the footage of the marches: a stressed but also ambivalent, even disinterested, relation between the banner and its bearers. I don't think the banner marches cohere. That is perhaps part of how a socialist form, or perhaps more generally an authoritarian form, is inhabited anarchically. Or, to put it in another way, how a form of declaration becomes something more open-ended.

JS —— The open-ended work of art. It's easy to desire, but it's something I fear as well. I've been lecturing more lately than I have for years, which means I've been forced to try to articulate 'positions' on a number of things. While not teaching, I could just coast along, making work and hoping it would be strong enough to create sufficient response in viewers for me to be able to become one of them. I always liked it that way. You make something and when it's finished you change your position towards it from being its maker to being just another of its viewers. And you make sure you're not a lone viewer—that is, you exhibit. In the crowd, you hear different ideas about what this 'thing' means. You listen, propose, discuss, collect—but your 'answer' doesn't carry any more authority than anyone else's. It can be a great joy to be one of the crowd, but at the same time there are situations where you have to try to clearly articulate why you made this 'thing' exactly this way and not another. What drove your decisions? It's not a free-for-all, obviously, because if it were, nothing would have been finished, or there would have been any number of alternative versions to the finished work. So what is it that made you, the artist, the maker, do what you did in exactly the way you did it? And where does your responsibility end regarding the way the product of these decisions is interpreted? The random production of art never works, so I believe a truly open work of art is an oxymoron.

Two loosely related thoughts:

(1) Yesterday I listened to the writer Khaled Hosseini discuss his book *The Kite Runner* in front of a live BBC audience. He was asked the following question by a young writer who said he'd recently been short-listed for the 'Muslim Writers Award':

> How can you, as a Muslim writer who has made it into the mainstream, use your characters and your story to alter perceptions about Islam?

Having first congratulated the questioner for being short-listed, and then wished him luck for his writing career (a gesture which

I thought both pleasant and professional), Hosseini gave an answer which included:

> I think that if you set out with a goal to change perceptions, you're doomed to fail. I think people will read through that.

(2) Back in 1975, the Ramones wrote a song called 'Today Your Love, Tomorrow the World'. The lyrics go like this:

> *I'm a shock trooper in a stupor / Yes I am*
> *I'm a Nazi schatze / Y'know I fight for the fatherland*
> *Little German boy / Being pushed around*
> *Little German boy / In a German town*
> *Today your love, tomorrow the world*[1]

I always loved this song, and while I was fascinated by the lyrics, I also felt some distance from them. In art school I made a piece using the same title. The other day I bought a Ramones tribute CD, and the last track is an intriguing version of 'Today Your Love, Tomorrow the World'. It sounds like it's sung by John Frusciante from the Red Hot Chili Peppers, but there are no credits for the track, neither on the label nor on the cover. In this version, the song is played slowly on acoustic guitar, and sung plaintively, with an accompanying celestial choir. The singer repeatedly uses an altered version of the first line: 'I'm a Nazi, baby / a Nazi, yes I am'. Joey Ramone (who was Jewish) was also known to have performed this version in concert. Sung in earnest, the effect is outright eerie; I can't shake it off.

TN —— I would tend towards the inverse: the closed work of art as oxymoronic. I can't think of an artwork I like which is not, in some deep-seated sense, open. But to me this is different to the work manifesting a position or not.

The banner marching began through a vaguely conceived visual question: what happens to the form of the banner, and the activity of banner marching, when you strip the banner of its declaration, its overt inscription? As I continued to make the banners, organize the marches, and film the unfolding of these actions, I became increasingly interested in the messiness, tensions, even nonsensical nature of the marches. As I revisited the footage of the marches, I began to include dimensions of the actions I had previously edited out: the moments when the marches cease to function smoothly, the sometimes awkward relation between the marchers and the photographers, the various physical impediments and unforeseen blockages which the marchers encounter, the sheer difficulty of handling the banners. But even in the attitude I developed towards the end of the life of the project —allowing into the work what the actions 'collected' serendipitously, and often against my planning and pre-decisions—the work articulated a kind of position, I think. The open-endedness *is* a position—a position against instrumentalised action, a position in search of a kind of public action which might be read, at least at the level of a fleeting proposition, with the same complexity as an interesting picture. This was partly trying to encompass the spectrum of meanings embodied in the diverse range of image-bearing rituals—commemorative pacifist actions (like the Chilean relatives of activists 'disappeared' during the Pinochet years), dissident left-wing protest (like Trade Union banners in Melbourne), state sponsored parades (like the Soviet-style banner marches), fascist or militarist rituals (like The Twelfth, the Protestant marches in Northern Ireland), or religious marches (like the annual Volto Santo ritual in Lucca). The decisions I made as the work evolved were an attempt to encompass these disparate meanings, to confuse the memorial and the forward-looking, the retrospective and prospective.

To respond to your question in a more general sense, I tend to think that the openness of a work of art is not a way to sit on the fence. It is the way it generates meaning, its complexity, its density. It provides a feeling that the work can't be encountered with any finality. Didactic art gets a hard run when political art is discussed, but I actually think there are some great didactic artworks. *The Last Judgement* in the Sistine Chapel is a profoundly didactic work. So is Goya's *The Disasters of War*. But they are extraordinarily complex in the ways they generate meanings and in their relation to lived visual experience. The demands they make upon our looking and thinking is their openness, the sense they do not foreclose or exhaust themselves. The open work of art unsettles our sense of resignation—in our living, and specifically in the habits of our perceiving—because it resists its own closure.

JS —— I should clarify that the 'positions' I speak about formulating might well have very short lives, before being replaced. In stereotypical German art-speak, artists are assumed to stake out 'eine Position' for themselves (as soon as possible!), and to be always ready to defend it (much like the quintessential German tourist with his towel on the beach). This territorial idea always irritated me immensely. I became an artist to explore my freedom, not to imprison myself. On the other hand, a closed structure without a prisoner can have a lot going for it.

I'd propose there are closed artworks which might be quite productive in generating viewer activity…

I once used the metaphor of a fortified

city deserted by its citizens. The heavy gates have been locked from the outside. The keys thrown back in, over the wall. Later, we arrive and gaze in wonder at this impregnable fortress, making various assumptions about what we would find inside should we ever gain entry.

Of course, it's of the utmost importance that we never do.

You edit your film after the march has taken place, and focus on the 'other' stuff collected around the event, because your footage of the event itself remains mute. It's like one of my imagined travellers sitting on a hill overlooking the impregnable city, then temporarily shifting his attention from the centre to the periphery because what's in the centre seems immobile. In the next moment, though, this might change. No-one knows. The uncertainty creates a tension. Tension forces a higher level of consciousness.

Regarding the Sistine Chapel … today I read an essay by one of my Helsinki students. In it he argues that *The Last Judgement* can be seen as an ornament. Can it be both didactic and ornamental?

TN —— I like your metaphor (the terrifying image of the German tourist at the beach wielding towels involuntarily brought to mind Joseph Beuys and his blackboards).

To follow up on that image of scantily

dressed or nude bodies with towels, I don't think *The Last Judgement* is 'ornamental', which to me is a pejorative label, suggesting a form stripped of its associations, its richness, and reduced to a kind of patterning. The forms in that work are characterized by a great density of associations, which is in part how the work exceeds its didactic message (i.e. 'you will go to hell, just like this, if you are bad'). That excess is partly their formal complexity. The frontality of the wall's position in the chapel 'grips' the frontality of the image, the way the bodies are configured to dramatically face us, face us off. And this 'gripping' relates the imagined weight of those figures and the huge vertical expanse of the wall itself (a relation which is encoded morally and existentially). Those forms also exceed their didactic function through their relation to lived experience, the power with which Michelangelo's bodies evoke the weight, sensation, coiled muscularity, sag and pleasure of the human body. These are experiences we all know in a profoundly 'felt' way and, for me, they are a crucial element of the latent secular dimension of the work. The density of these associations creates something like your fortress—something which compels us, which we necessarily encounter through our imaginative faculties, but which resists any final, authoritative perception.

At the risk of being too literal, one of the

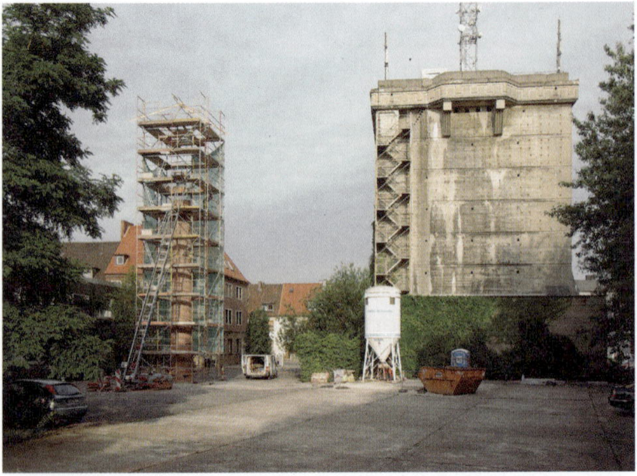

The Ninth Chimney in construction, Hamm, Germany, 25 June 2008.
Photograph: Jan Svenungsson.

things which has always struck me about
your chimneys is their physical closure. 28, 62
They have an interior, but one that cannot be
entered, at least once the building process is
complete. This sense is amplified by the nar-
rowness of that interior space, and the chim-
ney's immensely laborious and physically
strong or resistant material construction. 26
All those bricks. Such a fortress, containing
that little cigarette of dark space.

JS —— The artist who described Michelan-
gelo's painting as ornamental was not trying
to lessen its value. Quite the opposite. He's
on a mission to re-assign value to ornament
and to the ornamental impulse. His current
project is building his own house according 30
to these ideas, a project in which I play a
small part, even though I have more affinity
with 'the enemy', i.e. the empty-space-loving
modernist.

In terms of *The Last Judgement*, it's interesting to ponder whether both of you might be right. Could a composition (could art in general) whose primary function is/was to make more beautiful a surface and thereby enliven a space, simultaneously create this density of associations of which you speak—all the while aspiring to the mute draw of my deserted, locked-up fortress town? I think history has replied in the affirmative, many times. Interestingly, this insight is not

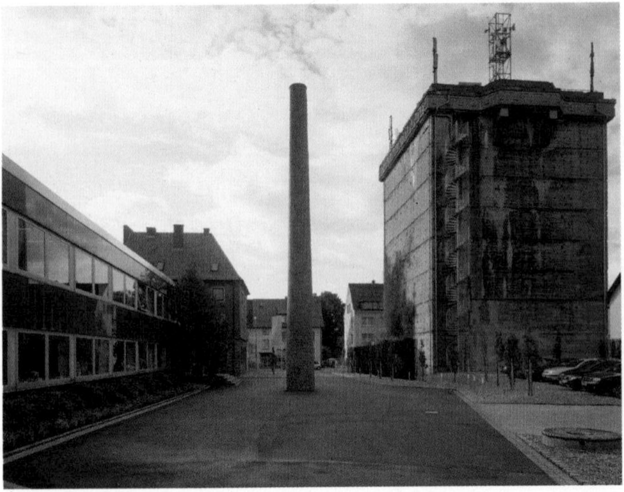

Jan Svenungsson, *The Ninth Chimney*, brick and mortar, 18 m, Jäckering company grounds, Hamm, Germany 2008. Photograph: Jan Svenungsson.

enough to make me want to introduce ornaments into my house. In my private sphere I aim for random emptiness (in contrast to contrived minimalism and designerism). Nevertheless, in my professional activity as a sometime builder of vertical brick structures, I have a laborious program for producing precisely defined, narrow, conical, empty, sealed-off spaces. Absolutely not random, they are pre-planned, controlled—but not didactic. Even so, they aim to encourage erratic thoughts and associations, haphazard reflection, accidental conclusions. That was always my desire. As well as fear, naturally.

TN —— I find it hard not to use the word
'decorative' in a pejorative sense (and I am
guilty of the same reflex with the word 'for-
malism', which as a body of ideas and work is
as heterogeneous as the decorative). Perhaps
the ornamental is something slightly dif-
ferent, but there are certainly cases where a
decorative work is not an emptying out of
meaning, but precisely its charge. I wonder
if that Emily Kam Kngwarray painting we
viewed together at the National Gallery here
in Melbourne, *Big Yam Dreaming*, could 32
rightly be described as decorative or orna-
mental. I think we both agree about its
greatness as a picture (and hers as an artist).
In that work the decorative becomes a field
which seems to be the presence of the body,

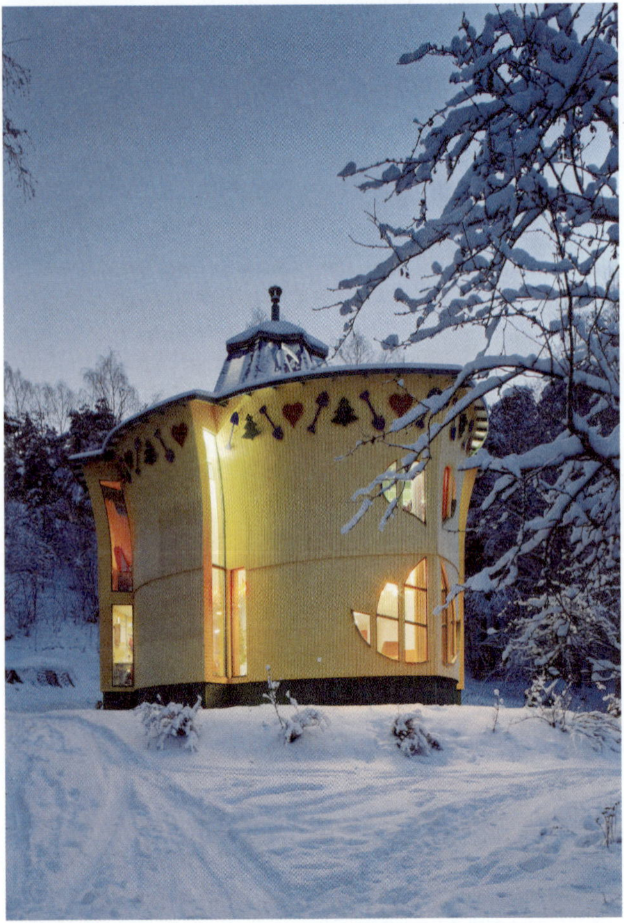

Jan-Erik Andersson: *Life on a Leaf*, one family house created in collaboration with architect Erkki Pitkäranta, Turku, Finland 1999–2010. Photograph: Matti A. Kallio.

the force of certain memories, and a landscape, in both an observed and secular sense, and in an imaginary and religious one. For me the work also reads in terms of an automatist tradition, or at least, I think it is clear it does not emerge from a process of composition (which would almost be impossible for an eight-metre-long work produced sitting 34
on the ground). Perhaps this is the sense in which it operates beyond the decorative, because of this automatism, with its implication of a secret—or something that cannot be consciously described—as the undercurrent of the surface.

JS —— Oh, that wonderful, wonderful painting! I think your reference to the automatic 'tradition' makes a lot of sense, at least as a point of departure for discussing what this thing, this black surface with white marks, could be. And what it means. It sure is a minefield, in a most positive sense (if such a confused metaphor can be allowed). I suppose we can agree that we can never know the degree to which the artist, while making the work, was aware of the ramifications of the context *for which* her work was destined. Concurrently it must be quite clear to us that we, on the other hand, will never be able to fully grasp the 'true' signification of the artist's marks, in the context *in which* she was operating. I could say, there is a double

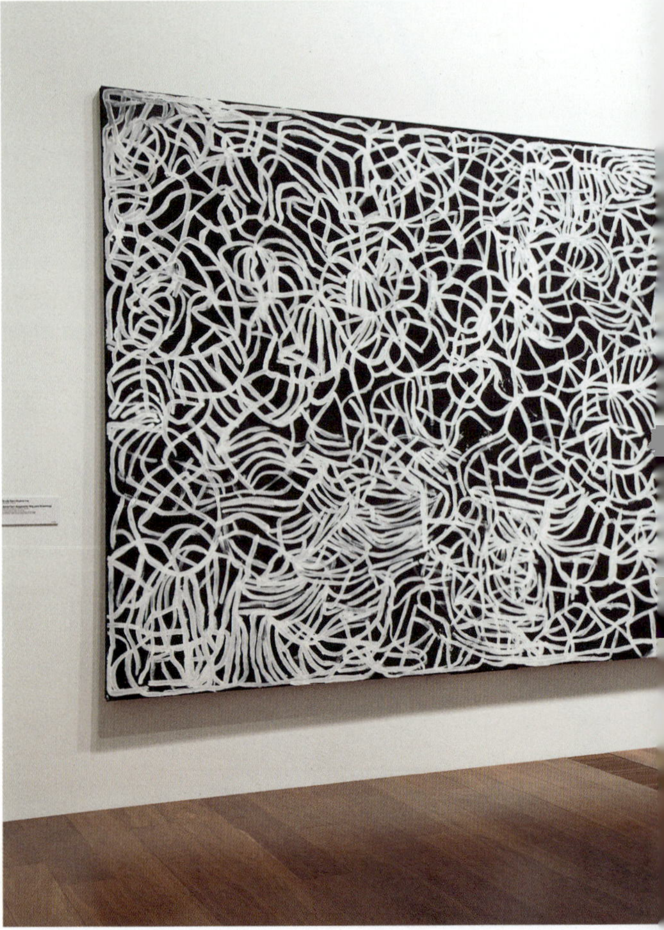

Emily Kam Kngwarray
Anmatyerr c.1910–1996
Anwerlarr anganenty (*Big Yam Dreaming*) 1995
synthetic polymer paint on canvas
291.1 × 801.8 cm
National Gallery of Victoria, Melbourne
Presented through The Art Foundation of Victoria
by Janet and Donald Holt and family, Governors, 1995
© Emily Kam Kngwarray / Licensed by Viscopy, 2011

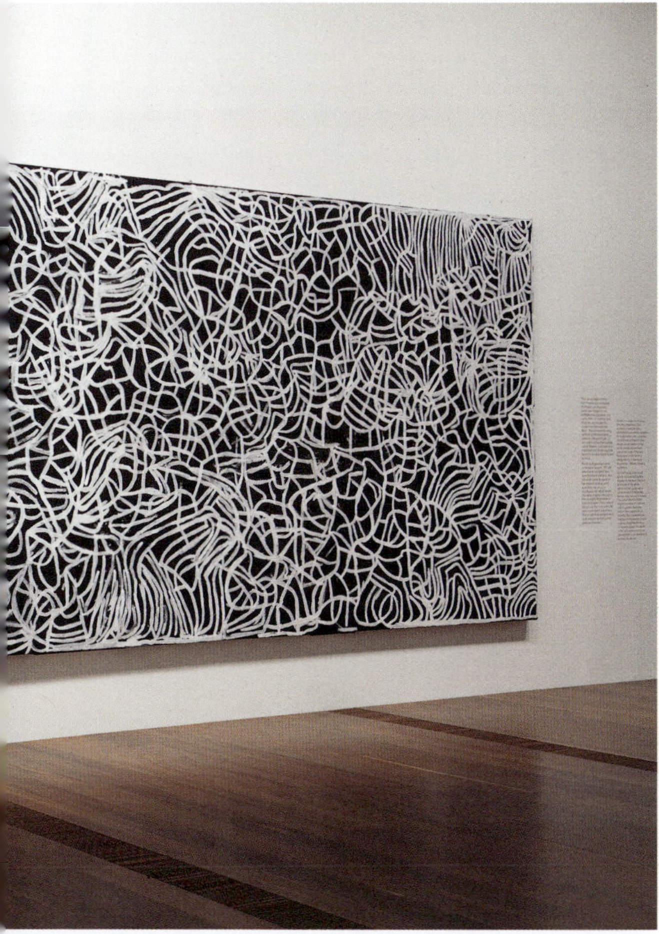

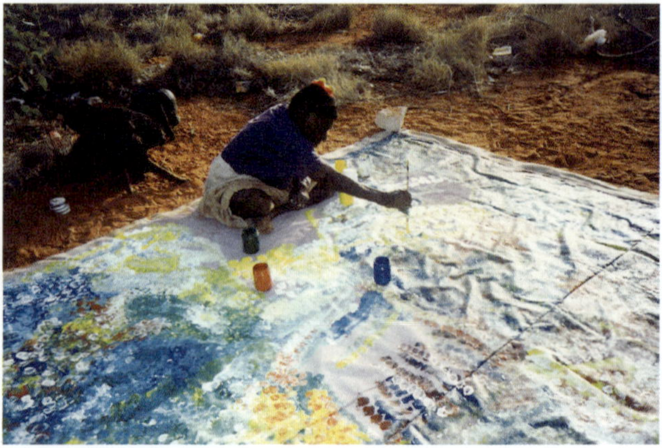

Emily Kam Kngwarray painting *Earth's Creation 1* at Utopia in 1994, 275 × 632 cm. Commissioned by DACOU. Photograph by Fred Torres.

automatism at work here, one in which the two parties are operating blindly, or in some trance. The artwork is the revelation, yes—but of what? And to whom? Perhaps what is being revealed with such force is the fact that once you begin to understand, nothing is left but secrets.

TN —— I think you're right. *Big Yam Dreaming* compels us through this 'double automatism', which also forms its strange 'public address'. What you say also links two components of your own work: your automatist
drawings (I am thinking here of your psycho- 38
mapping drawings) and the chimneys (which I think operate in a way not unrelated to the monumental secrecy of Emily's painting, the second sense in which you describe the work as automatist). I wonder if we can begin to use this terminology about works of art in the public sphere, like your chimneys, which are situated in public spaces yet are not simply the affirmation of their own context, but are, in fact, interruptions to the patterns of mainstream public visual language? Or, to put it another way, can we talk about an automatist 'public address'?

JS —— The impossible dream made true: content that comes to us from 'the other (side)'. Isn't it what we always wish for? I believe I do.

Now I will digress again.

I have just spent a few days in Stockholm, working with several men on the drawn-out installation of a public artwork in a square. Nights were spent at my parents' house. One evening I had a rather serious discussion with my father, a retired Lutheran bishop, about the concept of grace, God's grace. He at one point made a surprisingly straightforward (to me, at least) proposition that, in the end, it is *only* His grace which counts if a person is to achieve peace in the face of death. Preparation, piety, dedication, good deeds—ultimately, none of these matter. The way I understand him (correctly I hope, but I can't be sure), is that we are helpless but we can be helped—only if *God* chooses to. To me this sounds rather horrible, because if it doesn't matter what we do, and only some of us will be helped (which is clearly the case), what kind of dark humour makes God decide not to give grace to everyone?

The reason I bring this up here is that I, the atheist, feel profoundly disturbed by this idea of being at God's mercy. To my father, I tried to present an alternative understanding of the ultimate purpose and our quest for meaning, along the lines of 's/he who searches shall find', which I believe is also a sentiment expressed in the Bible.

How then does this all relate to my understanding of art? It's all very complicated, but again and again the art that I make expresses a yearning which I can see has parallels with what my father expressed. Certainly I spend a lot of effort trying to make things happen, yes, that's true, but ultimately I hold out hope for some sort of grace, something that will instil my art with *content that I have not consciously produced.*

The psycho-mapping drawing series tries to achieve this by way of a strictly regulated copy-of-a-copy-of-a-copy process, where 40
the imperfection of the human machinery (i.e. my eye and hand) keeps introducing little mistakes which, over the course of the series, accumulate and are amplified and eventually lead to a new vision coming into being. This vision (well, content, at least) is something I have worked against throughout the production of the work, as I tried at all cost to avoid, not to produce, mistakes.

The chimneys are set up differently, in that they are singular pieces which demand a huge investment both of money and of faith (in the work, not in God) on the part of the organizers of the exhibition. In the most recent case, such faith was required of the private collector, an industrialist, who has let me build my *Ninth Chimney* (18 metres 26, 28
high) directly in front of his two-storey 1960s office building in Hamm, Germany. Looming over both office and chimney is a 26-metre-high WW2 bunker with the famous

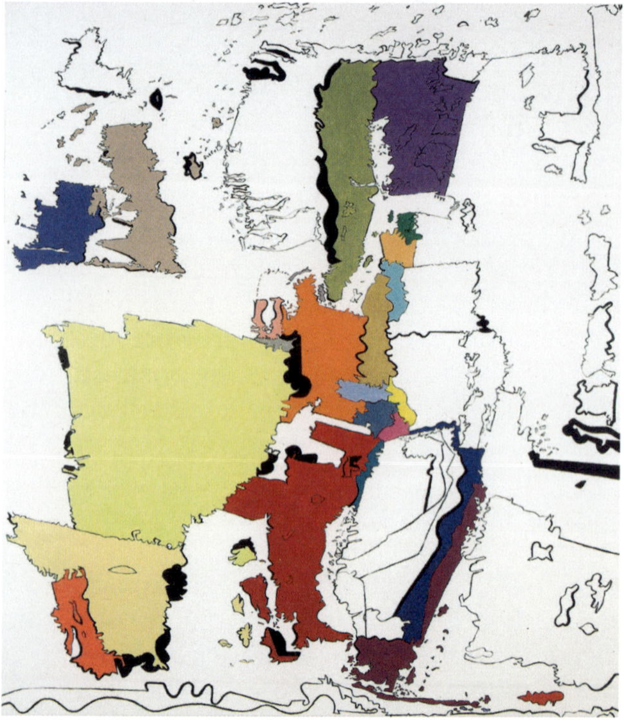

Jan Svenungsson, *Psycho-Mapping Europe version 2.0 – 22*, oil on canvas 190 × 165 cm, 2009. Private collection, Stockholm. Photograph: Jan Svenungsson.

'Hitler Balcony' still intact.[2] It's a very potent combination, scary and exhilarating. Scary because of all the obvious iconographic and historical connections that can be made. Exhilarating because of all the connections that *will* be made, which are not obvious. It's like with Emily's painting: I'm in at the deep end and the collector doesn't really know what he's getting, and I certainly don't *know* what I am giving. In possible contrast to my father's position, I think it's really important that I've given lots of attention to all the details of the project which were visible, accessible to me. But maybe my position comes closer to him than it should, when, in the end, I give the interpretative efforts of everyone equal status, and thereby hope for some sort of grace.

TN —— At the beginning of this exchange, as you described our walk around those incredibly arresting (and nose-numbingly cold) empty spaces of Suomenlinna, you mentioned a work you made for a gallery space on that island which was generated by the random processes of a computer. In many of your works I find something like a longing for the negation of one's self and the liberation this paradoxically provides. I even detect this desire in the process of bricklaying with your chimney project—that the constituent element of the work, at least in

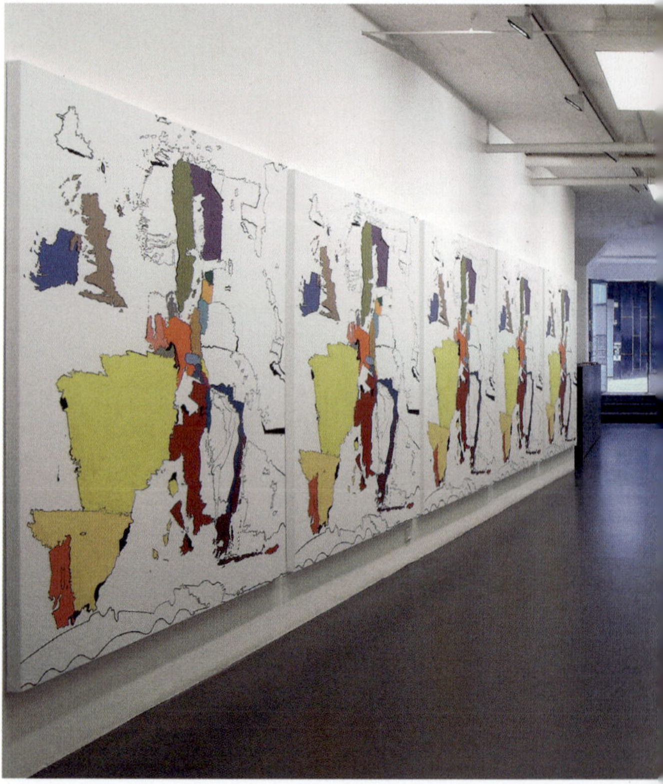

Installation view of *Psycho-Mapping Europe version 2.0*, 20 paintings in oil on canvas, each 190 × 165 cm, 2007–2009, collection: Malmö Konstmuseum, Malmö, Sweden. Installed in Galleri Flach+Thulin, Stockholm, 2009. Photograph: Jan Svenungsson.

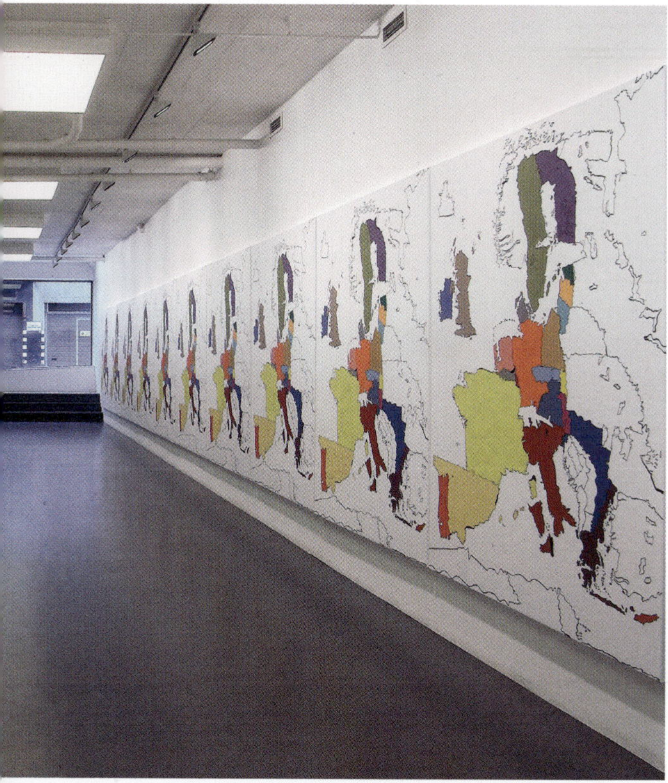

physical and optical terms, is impersonal, repeated, and organized in a pre-determined way (as well as involving a certain kind of labour which one could crudely connect to a protestant ethic). I am curious to follow the line of thought you have begun, excavating how your father's theological position might manifest itself surreptitiously in your own work. As I sift through remembered experiences of your work, I think there is an insistent presence which is invoked by this consistent self-negation, or attempts at self-negation. But this presence strikes me as very deeply secular—one which asserts the primacy and richness of both our sensation and our agency as material beings. There is a nagging in the psycho-mapping drawings which is *from* or perhaps *to* the body—not your body, but a body. And specifically to the wonder of the body to sense, judge, feel and act. These are all reconciled through memory, which for me is the zone that your self-negation activates, even as the works themselves rely upon the unreliability of memory as the principle of their formal evolution. This, I think, is the bind of those works, that they exalt the kinds of knowledge that accumulate in the body even as their process utterly constrains how these accumulations might be expressed as decisions. I have the feeling that the secrecy of the chimneys as forms draw upon the same zone, though they do so within the paradoxical conditions of public art, as a form which occupies our shared space and is beheld by many people at once, but which seems to both emanate and address the knowledge our bodies accumulate as memories, a space where sensations gather but cannot be readily accessed. Whereas the psycho-mapping drawings seem to be designed to be looked at in a way that echoes the solitary nature of their creation, or even the solipsism of the process, the chimneys are public works. Although in one sense they are aggressive intrusions into space—and classically monumental in their phallic structure—I think what is delicate in their public address is the sense in which they find their voice through what accumulates through and into our bodies. And that is a part of their connection to the chimney drawings which you make alongside this project—that even as the chimneys assume the form of a public declaration, their open-endedness seems to be animated by a zone which, by its nature, is the point at which our public or collective identity frays.

JS —— Self-negation, yes. As you say, in my case it is a secular attitude. There is no meaning in life—or art—except the meaning we create. As a consequence, for me, it was always reassuring to have a pronounced element of manual labour as a necessary

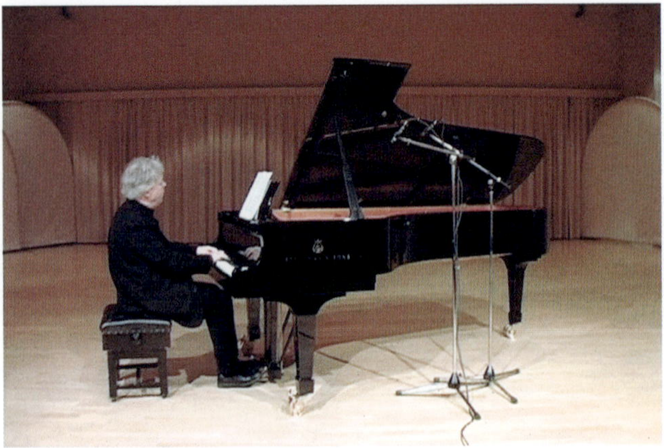

Jan Svenungsson, stills from *Concert*, video, 53 min, 2009. Renowned pianist Hans Pålsson plays a composition, by Jan Svenungsson, made by employing a random system of gradual repetition on a melody segment taken from the Swedish National Anthem.

step towards the realization of an artwork. There will be no artwork without an idea, but in my case the idea has to mature though a process of labour which can be seen as mindless. Still, I couldn't ask an assistant to make the psycho-mapping copies, and while the bricks for a chimney are laid by professionals, I would never build a chimney without taking an active part in the work as a labourer. I want to experience the *being there*, and I want my *having-been-there* to be a part of the finished work.

Could you imagine organizing a march in which you did not take part?

I don't deny that works (of art)—public work, also—can be perfectly relevant and valuable without the artist having felt the need for this kind of personal involvement. This investment is crucial for me though, and it is probably related to my being an atheist with a Protestant background. As your atheist convictions grow, you realize you're on your own. You're left with your 'self' to commune with. (Never mind that there are a lot of other selves out there; what counts is what is within you—in that place or space—where God is supposed to be.) Being alone is a fearful proposition, and one is open to ways to temporarily forget this status.

Why did *we* invent God—and why not any of the other millions of forms of beings that roam the earth? Easy: because we could. And

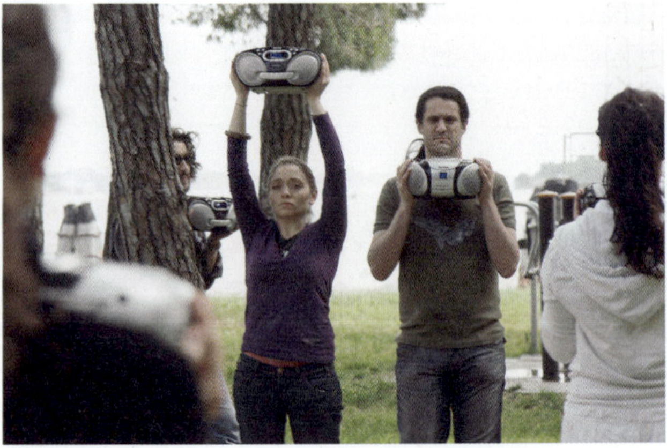

Andrew Byrne and Tom Nicholson, *Lines towards another century*, 2009. Instruction-based score for ten performers, recorded sound and voices, and ten boomboxes, 30 minutes. Performed by the contemporary music ensemble, L'Arsenale, auspiced by Media Art Bath, in the Parco delle Rimembranze, Venice, 6 June 2009. Photograph: Sam Nightingale.

Lines Towards Another Century was a part of an on-going collaboration between Nicholson and the New York-based composer Andrew Byrne. The work was structured around Nicholson's list of national boundaries created during the 20th Century, intoned by a single female voice. The recorded intoning of the list functioned as a kind of ordering system for the movement of the performers through the space of the Parco delle Rimembranze. Each performer remained silent, moving through the park, bearing the transmission of a recorded intoning, which ordered, prompted and contained their movements, creating layers and accumulations of sound.

because we could, we needed to. It's all the fault of language, which we invented first.

That's the true wonder.

TN —— Yes, language enables these inventions, though in some cases it feels like it dissembles them too. In the time since I mentioned Michelangelo's *The Last Judgement* I have been working in Prato in Italy and, on my way back to Melbourne, I spent a few days in Rome. Clare and I spent an afternoon in the Sistine Chapel (at the same time wrestling two children under 2, a task which at times seemed to resemble the apocalyptic wrestling taking place in the image on that big end wall). Through the good fortune of having lived in Italy on several occasions, I have spent quite a lot of time with those frescos, but I was still taken aback by seeing them again—that rush through the heart and into the guts that my body strangely produces when the eyes begin to apprehend something as great as those images. Apart from the sheer visceral quality of that response—a kind of pleasurable physical shock which, in a brief moment, clarifies the need we have for art—I found myself dwelling on a number of thoughts. I contemplated the strange echo between the Old Testament flooding scene on the ceiling and *The Last Judgement* on the end wall, in a narrative sense, moments of reckoning and cleansing, and in a formal sense, bodies dislodged into strangely shallow and undifferentiated fields. I was drawn to the extreme complexity of the patterning of the ceiling—a set of formal rhythms, shifting spaces and hues which my eyes felt happy to travel across and into endlessly—and Adam's passive pose, awaiting God's finger, the compression of that critical moment into such a small piece of meterage on that huge expanse of ceiling. And I found myself thinking about Michelangelo's images of God. Though the wise, powerful, bearded patriarch is such a familiar personification of God, I still found myself looking at the pictures of that buff, grey-haired man and thinking it was odd. It may be my Protestant heritage coming back to haunt me as a set of limitations to my imaginative faculties (and is there a place on earth where a Protestant feels more Protestant than in Rome?), but Michelangelo's language seems to consume his putative theology. Or more precisely, his visual language is so invested in the complexity of the human that it overcomes his attempt to picture a presence beyond us. This possibility, that language enacted can push beyond our overtly declared beliefs, is one of the great powers of art, and is perhaps another way of describing what you are talking about when you say you want to generate 'content that one will not consciously have produced oneself'. But it makes for a funny bind for artists who try to describe God. An image conceived to describe His power ends up exalting, and manifesting, a countervailing power, language, or at least the concentration of language into an artwork.

JS —— For three days in a row we have been to dinner with Tacita Dean, who has a big show of new work at the Villa Oppenheim and at a gallery. Yesterday was the high point. Her most fervent admirer, a dealer from London, had teamed up with a friend here in Berlin who lives in an exquisitely renovated Shell gas station surrounded by a Chinese garden, in Kreuzberg. In Tacita's honour they offered her and her choice of 30 friends a fantastic home-cooked dinner that ended with brie cheese ice-cream. The dealer-host had transported his collection of Tacitas here, just for this dinner, to surround us with them. The gas station-host didn't even eat his own dinner, so busy was he cooking for us. It was an extraordinary evening, marked by the most touching generosity—all of it ultimately motivated by something Tacita is able to do in her art, using the power of the language she is commanding—which is different from Michelangelo's. But how different?

At one point I overheard the dealer-host talking to her about the piece in her show

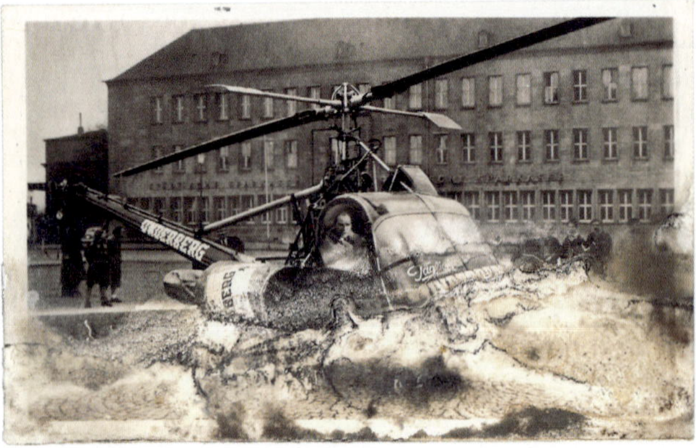

Tacita Dean, *Found Damp* (*Helikopter*), found postcard, plastic holder, 30.5 × 35.5 cm framed, 2008. Courtesy of the artist, Frith Street Gallery, London and Marian Goodman Gallery, New York / Paris.

that he most coveted—I think he will go through fire to get it! (It's possibly my favourite as well.) What is it? A found postcard of 50
a helicopter heavily damaged by damp conditions. A postcard found by the artist at a flea market, not touched or in any physical way altered. But completely changed by thought: invested with her love of 'objective chance', and now powerful in a way which defies description.

TN —— I don't know that work by Tacita, but your description reminds me of an economy that I have occasionally encountered—a great work generated by the simple act of finding, the only intervention an act of (dis)placement. By way of example, I am thinking of a body of work I first encountered through a dinner *you* hosted, at which I first met the artist Călin Dan, whose work through the collaborative entity subREAL I very much admire. It is that wonderful body of work comprising documentation of 52, 54, 56
Romanian official sculpture taken from the archive of the Romanian state art journal, but with the people holding the white or black sheets behind the sculptures kept in the frame, not cropped out as they were when the photographs were originally published in the journal. That was simply an act of noticing something, an act of imagining an image differently to its intended purpose.

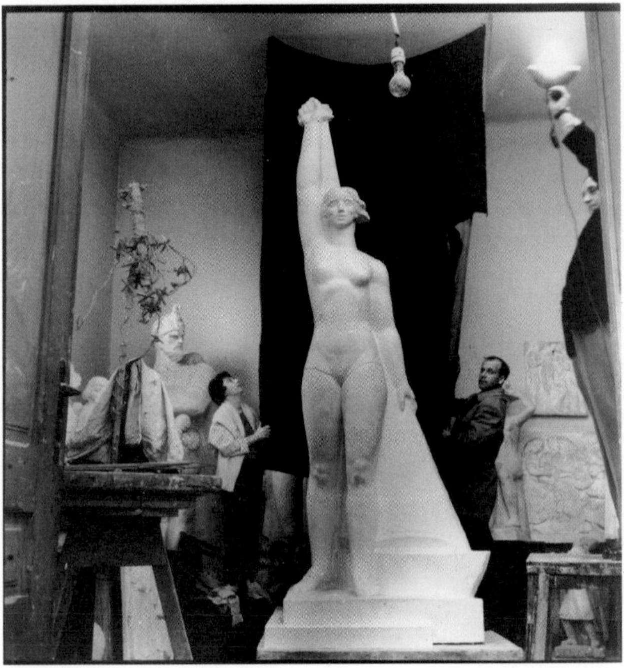

Above, and pages 54 & 56:
subREAL, *Serving art*, 1960s–1997, black and white photographs, 18 × 24 cm each.
Courtesy of Călin Dan and Iosif Kiraly.

The transformation of those photographs was achieved simply by a shift in their circulation, by an act of placement into a new context, conceiving those images as readymade artworks. Their force is located at the margins of the images, within a space of inadvertent form-making which photography allows—and which, in those images, sets itself against the usually pre-determined *and over-determined* meanings of the sculptures, whose documentation is the purpose and centre of the image. The absence of intervention by subREAL—other than through seeing, imagining, transforming by a decision of circulation—is part of the power of those pictures, their lightness, their opposition to the weight and authority of official art. That is also part of their peculiar 'public address'. They take that official, published art-making and 'create' a highly idiosyncratic and moving archive of anonymous people within that society, absorbed in a banal task—a portraiture of brief unremembered moments. Most of the public art that litters our cities—and here I have in mind the shared failure of mediocre nineteenth-century monuments in Melbourne and Berlin—fails by virtue of the heavy hand of too many obvious decisions, the necessity of an unambiguous public address, every detail carefully orchestrated to exclaim in unison. The lightness of touch in a body of work like subREAL's (and perhaps

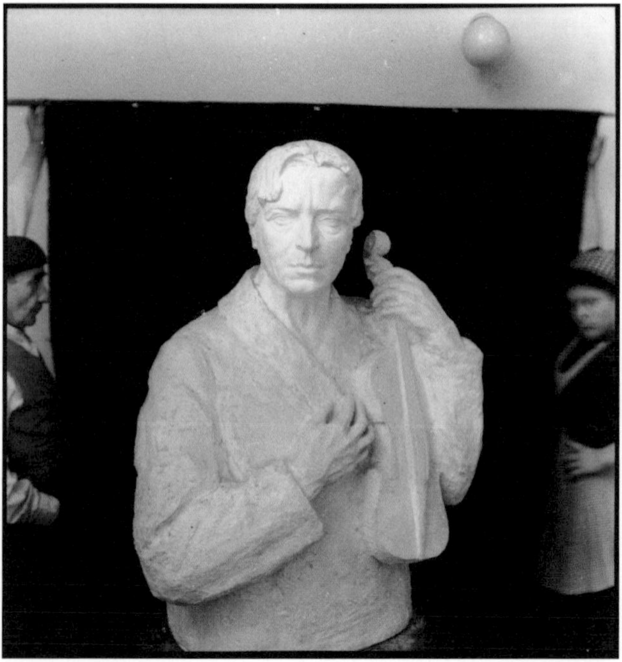

also in the work by Tacita you are describing) is an economy of transformation that only thinking possesses. In those subREAL photographs, that economy of transformation, that lightness of thinking, becomes linked to the shared spaces of our collective experience, not simply the private realm of daydreams and speculations.

JS —— I have been mulling over my instalment for several days already. I could have written it immediately, but I got distracted and then blocked by other things, so I have tried to make sense of the thoughts in my head before committing anything to paper (er, screen). I'm not sure it has helped! Most often, writing (and re-writing) *is* the thinking process. I don't understand those authors who know how the novel will end before starting on the opening chapter.

My trigger now is a certain uneasiness with my own instinctive love of the readymade—exemplified by my mention of Tacita's piece, and your mention of the subREAL works that I know well (and like), and lots of my own work as well. I would like to draw some sort of wider parallel with how we—by which I mean not us two now, but we in the contemporary world of art—have been addicted to the readymade since at least the early 1980s. The artist's gesture is now dominated by context, and the act of art has

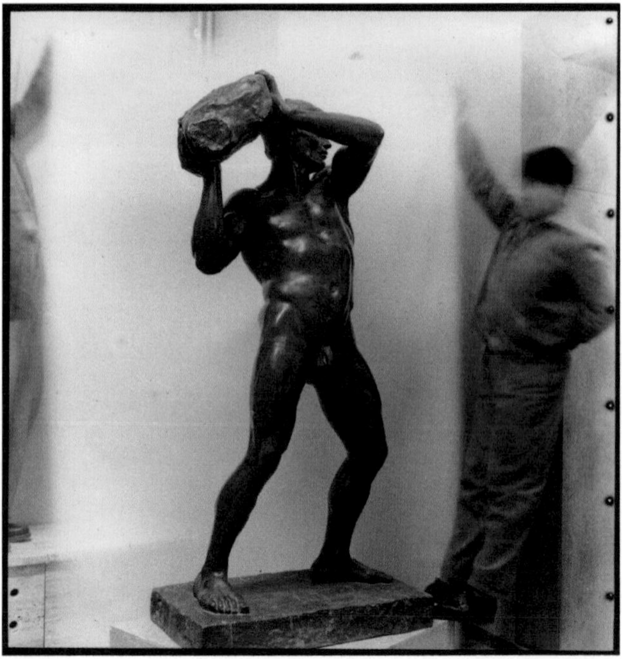

become, fundamentally, an act of language. Thank you Marcel! Or maybe not.

This observation, which is an observation of myself as well as of my surroundings, can give me a hint of nausea, even on a good day. It's the lack of a foundation in the production of a new visual form which disturbs me. All around us, right now in early December 2008, societies are shaking with the reverberations of the financial crisis triggered earlier this year by the collapse of financial instruments that had become so abstract that nobody any longer fully understood them. The other day, I imagined that one could develop a parallel analysis about the function of the readymade mechanism in contemporary art ... but I'm not the man to do it. And I don't think this analysis would trigger a similar crash in the art world.

The readymade remains a fundamental mechanism, both in the art I make and in an important percentage of the art that attracts me. That said, at the party for Tacita, I also found (and then received as a gift) a catalogue of an artist who was new to me: Alexander Ross. He makes pictures which look like representations of strange algae, but which are completely invented and are presented in a crisp, idiosyncratic visual language very clearly his own. I found this power to 'make it new' extremely refreshing. I'd like to be an artist like Ross, but I know I can't be.

Just to pile it on, I have to tell you we went to Hamburger Bahnhof's gigantic Beuys exhibition last Sunday. I wish you could have been there with us. It would have been great to discuss it with you, there, in front of the pieces. I'm afraid I'll confirm your suspicion of my bad manners by admitting that I really did not take to the exhibition at all. I found the attitude expressed over the course of the show really scary. The political project in particular. There's a poster explaining the advantages of direct democracy over representative democracy. Okay, there are some sensible points to this argument. However, combined with the overriding presence of Beuys' persona in the exhibition, I suddenly saw the attraction that a free-for-all situation presents for a leader with charismatic power. You get rid of all formal structures (through violence, desperation or art...), in order to create the most fertile ground for charismatic leaders, and only for them. Their names can be Beuys or Mugabe or Hitler... Their manifestos can be long, leaden and unreadable (of which I saw some good examples), because it is not the content that counts, but the power of presentation and persuasion.

Finally, there was that famous sentence (which, incidentally, I agree with): 'Das Schweigen von Marcel Duchamp wird überbewertet'.[3] Only, I would like to add a coda: 'Das Quatschen von Beuys ebenso'.[4]

TN —— I have just been reading a review of the Buckminster Fuller show at the Whitney in the *New York Review of Books*. I thought of Beuys, and the susceptibility of that era to charismatic visionaries/charlatans like Fuller and Beuys. As you know, my interest in Beuys is partly my ability/weakness to look past the rhetorical content of the work and to read it formally. I don't mean reading him in formalist terms, but through the ways the work's formal structure manifests political relations, specifically between the mnemonic and the propositional, the retrospective and the prospective. There is a bombast in a lot of his overtly political work which is fairly repellent (in this respect the poster *La revoluzione siamo noi*, with him striding towards the camera, surely takes the cake—not even the visual machinery of the USSR could manage such failed seriousness). Beuys' failures are sometimes comical (like his attempts to deliver his Lecture actions in English in the early 1970s), though I also think there are moments when he allows for that slippage into comedy, like his participation in singing 'Sonne Statt Reagan', or one of his most interesting multiples, *Demokratie ist lustig*, where humour becomes the expression of opposition to the authoritarian state. In many works, no such self-deprecating humour is allowed in, but I also think this earnestness functions powerfully in particular works. *7,000 Oaks*—an exemplary work of grand seriousness—is a great work, a meditation on the monument and on related processes of formal dispersal and social linkage. Beuys borrowed from Duchamp's idea of the readymade in a variety of ways (and always with the need to kill the father, which is how my own teacher at art school, Bernhard Sachs, understood that statement about Duchamp's silence, and I agree with him). Beuys' use of the oak tree at once adopts the readymade *as a process* through his use of the growth of the tree, against the massive readymade immobility of each corresponding basalt block, and also vests the work's meaning in the invisibility of this process. It does the latter in two senses: one, because we can't see the tree grow, except with the aid of time-lapse photography; and two, because the mechanics of its growth lie in an inside we do not see. This is part of the secrecy of that work, its particular mode of address, to history and to public space.

JS —— Yes, I like the oaks as well. Beyond the actual concept, the act of planting trees will always be a beautiful, imaginative thing to do. The next time I'm in Kassel I should go and see what has become of these trees. Oaks grow slowly!

It's funny, in the two years preceding Beuys' tree planting project in 1982, I was in a 'post-punk' group called Svart, and trees were a recurring theme in many of the lyrics I wrote for us. There was even a song called 'Under Träden' ('Under the Trees'). Another referred to trees in the Jardin du Luxembourg and another still to the wide forests of the north. Trees are peaceful beasts.

Writing this I feel some unease, because it makes me realize I have not been in contact with either you or any of my other Melbourne friends since the great fires devastated the Victorian bush. You sent me 64
your last instalment before they started. Many have died—trees and people. Have you seen the flames? Seen what remains? Fire dreamings by Clifford Possum and Tim Leura come before my eyes. Time to plant new trees.

TN —— That danger is part of the eucalypt. Its oily aroma is beautiful, but also indicates this danger—its extreme flammability. I don't feel this foreboding in a tree like the oak, which in Beuys' work contains the idea of redemption, embodies a process against destruction. The photographs of that huge wedge of basalt blocks in front of the Fridericianum, which slowly dispersed as the 7,000 oaks were planted around Kassel, always remind me of photographs of Kassel immediately after the war, its rubble-strewn streets. In *7,000 Oaks* the tree performs

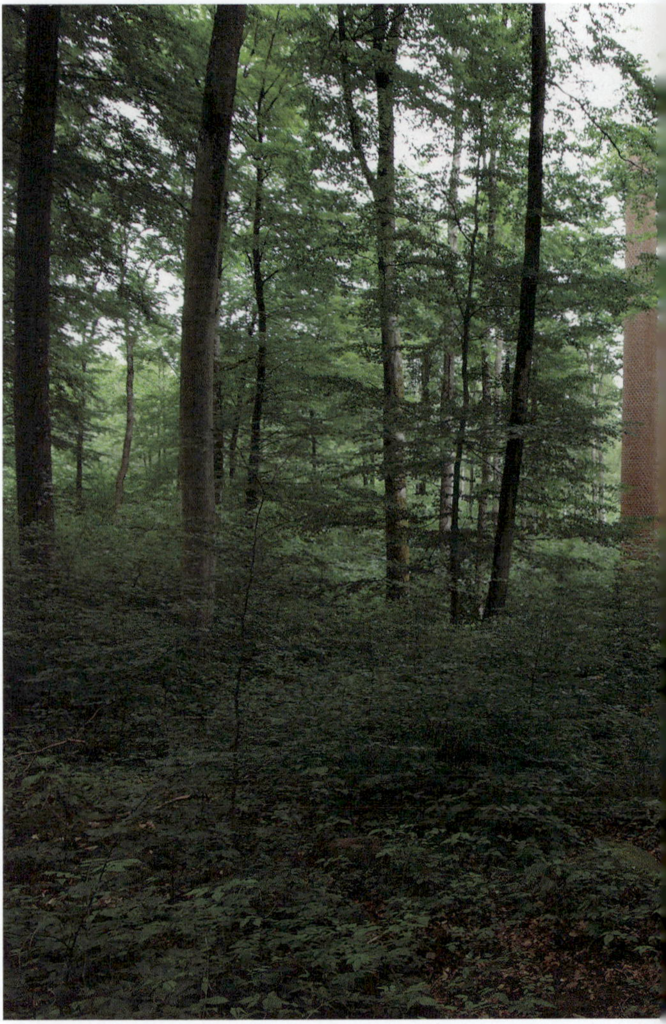

Jan Svenungsson, *The Eighth Chimney*, brick and mortar, 17 m, 2007.
Wanas Foundation, Knislinge, Sweden. Photograph: Jan Svenungsson.

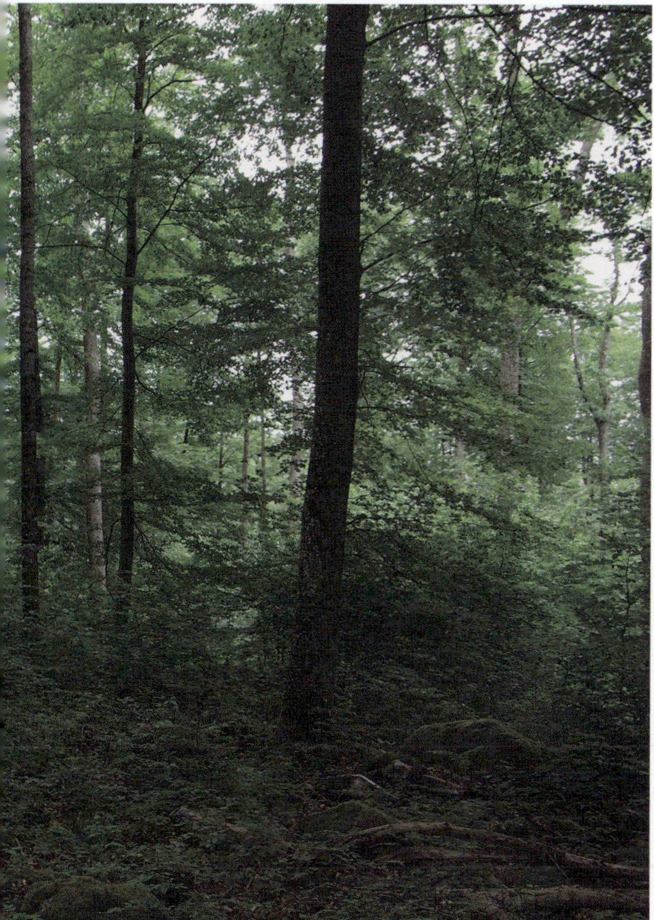

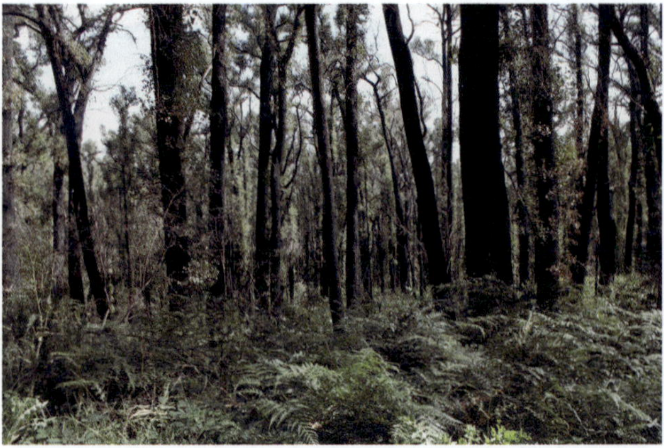

Charred eucalyptus trees between Healesville and Marysville, Victoria, 20 April 2010.
Photograph: Jan Svenungsson.

something in memory of the war and specifically *against* the nature of fire.

It is curious we have ended up talking about extreme heat, given that this dialogue began with your descriptions of an extreme wintery cold. The weeks leading up to the bushfires around Melbourne this February included the hottest sequence of days since the European invasion. And the day on which the bushfires began was more than three degrees hotter than the previous hottest day on record—a jump that greatly exceeds the very small increments by which these records are normally surpassed.

On that day, Clare and I were at an outdoor wedding at the Melbourne Zoo, and there was a moment about 20 minutes into this very beautiful but extraordinarily hot occasion when the wind changed very dramatically and the temperature dropped from 46 down to the high 30s. (Never have the high 30s felt like such a relief—it was a memorable sensation.) What was terrible (and I am thinking of the old meaning of this word, Michelangelo's *terribilità*) was that it was precisely this moment, this dramatic shift in the wind, which resulted in the deaths of all those people. The fire turned around, and fuelled by this new wind, travelled at over 100km an hour, generating heat comparable to the heat of the first atomic bombs. That sense of relief we felt—which feels so vivid as a physical recollection of the skin—has for me become the point from which this disaster is imagined and remembered.

I am often amazed at the kinds of images that very quickly surface from disasters—amateur video footage of the tsunami, even as the water rushes around the feet of the person holding the camera, or mobile phone photographs of the suicide bombers in the London tube, taken by someone just a few metres away from the smouldering malfunction of the backpack explosives. The Victorian bushfires are rare for the almost complete absence of photographs from within the disaster. Partly this is because the fire caused extreme conditions of invisibility (many died in car crashes as they tried to escape, driving into other cars or trees). It was also because of the speed and all-enveloping nature of the fire. If you were close enough to the fire to be able to see it, you were close enough to be killed by its radiant heat. It didn't allow the distance which vision normally affords us, to see disaster without being in it. It left an imageless space in its wake.

I must admit I have been collecting
68 photographs of chimneys. Not your kind. Domestic ones. Your work has definitely made me tune into old industrial chimneys (of which there are many in Brunswick, the area of Melbourne where I live). I suspect

this has sub-consciously fed my interest in a specific (domestic) chimney, which William Buckley built for John Batman's house in the very early years of Melbourne's history. In fact it was the first European house built at the site we now call Melbourne. Buckley was the escaped convict who lived with the Wathaurung people (near present day Geelong) for thirty years, the European who most completely assimilated to Aboriginal life, and who then re-joined European society in the fledgling town of Melbourne in 1835. Batman is the man who is regarded as the 'founder' of Melbourne, who initiated a 'treaty' with the Wurundjeri people in 1835 in which they traded their land to his enterprise, the Port Phillip Association, for a few meagre objects (the treaty was either forged by Batman, or was something that was incomprehensible to the Wurundjeri conceptually, something Buckley himself pointed out). When the print media began to fill up with images of the communities destroyed by the Victorian bushfires this February, the newspapers were full of domestic chimneys, which classically (and ironically) are the only parts of houses which survive bushfires. As people returned to their houses they often erected Australian flags, which, in several images I have collected, stand next to free-standing chimneys. As an assertion about the way we occupy this place (very different

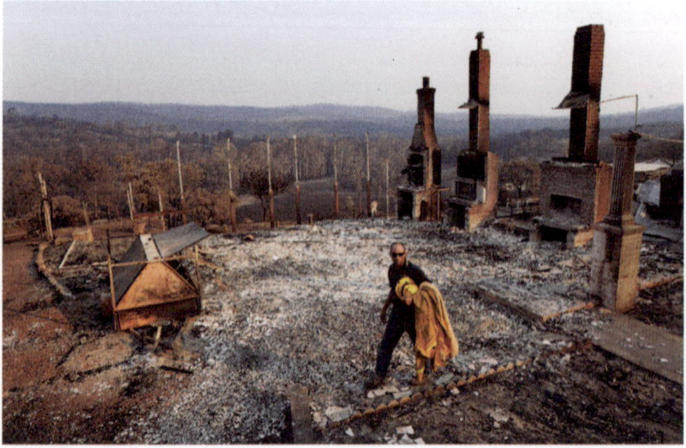

Photograph of firefighter Warren Rees in the ruins of his own house, destroyed during the Black Saturday fires. Photograph by Craig Borrow, first published in the *Herald Sun* on Thursday 19 February 2009, page 6. Reproduced courtesy of the Herald and Weekly Times.

to the way Aboriginal people inhabited the same land and dealt with the phenomenon of bushfire), the presence of the union jack on that Australian flag reminded me of that single chimney of ambiguous provenance, built by Buckley for Batman, and of a set of unresolved questions about sovereignty and the public visual languages that articulate them.

JS —— To hoist the flag beside the burnt-out remains of what was once your house is perhaps the most primary form of a public address. It speaks of survival, personal tenacity, and it raises the issues of ownership and belonging. I think, were we to be in that same situation, having seen (or rather, not seen, but *felt*, referring to your observation about the relationship between distance, view and survival) home and belongings annihilated in unbearable heat, we would also like to raise something, to prove (to ourselves?) our unbroken spirit. But what could it be? The national flag does seem a far-fetched option, I concur. What colour would my flag be? Not white or black. Perhaps not red, either. Blue? Green? Mellow grey? I'm not convinced, however, that in such a moment a statement of artistic poetry and ambiguity would seem right. I'm not keen to find out.

It seems increasingly likely that within our lifetimes we will come to see, and be personally touched by, catastrophes that will test our commitment to artistic ideas formulated in more peaceful times. Is the imageless space that followed the Victorian fires an aberration or a portent of things to come?

TN —— Yesterday I met up with two young East Timorese artists, Anata and Grinaldo, who are in Melbourne for an exhibition, and to participate in programmes at Monash (where I am a lecturer). They are art school students, but also teachers, at Arte Morris, a free art school that was set up by young East Timorese and a Swiss artist couple by squatting an old government building in Dili. About 25 artists—including Anata and Grinaldo—live and work in the building, teaching students as young as 14, who, if they show enough enthusiasm and aptitude, come to live there to keep studying and to join in with teaching the youngest students. Like everything in Timor, it is all done with little or no money, and with students for whom getting enough to eat is often a day-to-day proposition. I was talking to Anata and Grinaldo about the events of 2006, when severe factional and inter-regional violence rocked East Timor. They described how they were paid by the state to paint graffiti on the walls of the city, propaganda for peace and dialogue among the warring groups of youths. Such demands on their art-making are much more urgent than those on ours, but also more straight-forward, with much less space for speculation, for the open-endedness we have been talking about. I asked them what their parents thought about them and their colleagues becoming artists. They spoke of their impulse to make work, the necessity for creative spaces in a society. Anata quoted a conversation he had with his father in which he defended his life as an artist as a job, a daily activity. 'You look at your computer screen every day and I look at my canvas.' A very matter-of-fact affirmation of art—or, to paraphrase Anata more accurately, of the daily activity of making art—in the face of catastrophe and violence.

JS —— Getting on with it. You, me—we will continue making stuff we categorize as art. Because the need is there, within ourselves. This need is stimulated by discourse, but not dependent on it. Its roots lay deeper down, in the metaphysical fear and joy language once brought our surprised forebears. Just a couple of weeks ago there was an announcement about the discovery of what is now the most ancient work of art known to be in existence. It was found in a cave in Germany.[5]
It is 35,000 years old: a small, naked female 72
figure, with certain interesting distortions still popular in today's pornography. We're still there—we are still here.

exciting time for astronomy and physics. ■ pectations surrounding Alpha do not stem

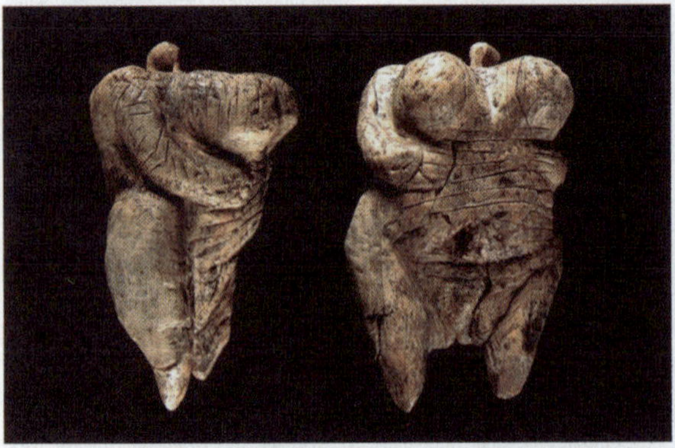

Palaeolithic pornography

From photography to the internet, a characteristic sign that a new medium is going to

Statue found in Hohle Fels Cave, Germany.
Photograph: Hilde Jensen, University of Tübingen.
As published in *The Economist*, 14 May 2010.

Nevertheless, what concerns us as individuals and artists now, is (again): how can we make what we do relevant, to us and to society? Some questions need always to be repeated.

TN —— It has been a while since I have written. And we have managed to see each other in person several times since then: in Sweden and in Italy twice, most recently in Venice. Perhaps this correspondence occurs at a pace inverse to the frequency with which we actually manage to see one another. For the most part, the work we saw at the Venice Biennale seemed remote from your last comments. In a way that was quite demoralizing, the work was mostly without that deep-seated 'need' to make things which you describe.

During my teaching in Prato over the last two months, unexpectedly, Fluxus became quite important to my conversations with the students. This was partly driven by a really wonderful presentation—part lecture, part concert—by Riccardo Vaglini, an Italian composer who works at the Venice Conservatorium but lives in Pistoia (close to Prato). Though Riccardo has a very well-established composing practice of a more conventional variety (i.e. not conventional music, but conventional scores), he is deeply interested in Fluxus music, and in particular in the late Florentine Fluxus artist Giuseppe Chiari.

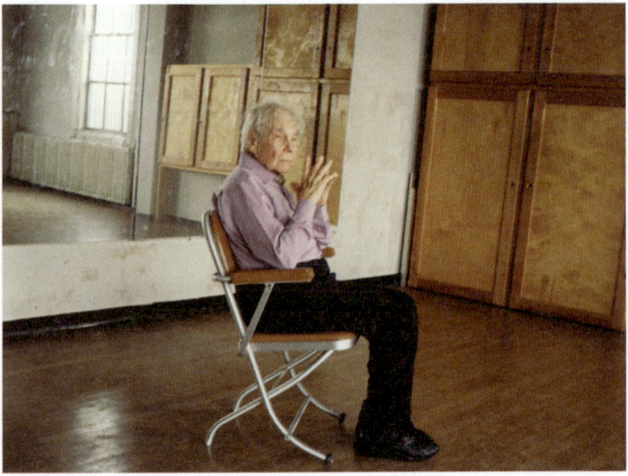

Tacita Dean, location photograph from *Merce Cunningham performs STILLNESS… (six performances, six films)*, 2008. Courtesy of the artist, Frith Street Gallery, London and Marian Goodman Gallery, New York / Paris.

Riccardo's presentation to my students in Prato concluded with a fantastic performance of Chiari's 'Musica madre', which Riccardo interprets as a score and involves a whole series of two-word alliterations with the word 'musica' ('musica mercato', 'musica merda', 'musica malinconia', 'musica mentire', 'musica mentre'). Riccardo does a wonderful, comic and charismatic performance of the work, which for me is beautiful not just for its simplicity, its swinging between the absurd and the heartfelt, but also for its conjoining of the iconoclastic-patricidal tropes of Fluxus (of which the physical destruction of that musical 'father', the grand piano, is perhaps Fluxus' best rehearsed example), and its expression of love and longing for music, for the joy, richness and necessity to make sense of sounds (which, in a way that I also think is very Italian, is figured through the image of the mother, 'madre').

The recurrence of Fluxus during my teaching made me remember a Tacita Dean work I saw at ACCA here in Melbourne several months ago (a memory conducted through an alliterated chain of artists Chiari-Cage-Cunningham). The work is a huge installation of 16mm projections, *Merce Cunningham* 74
performs STILLNESS (in three movements) to John Cage's composition 4'33", in which Cunningham appears in an otherwise empty dance studio, seated, almost completely

still. The projections are installed in such a way that it is almost impossible not to cast a shadow on one projection or another, so that in a very literal way, movement is constantly infecting the work's 'reaching' for stillness and silence. The work's accumulation of uncontrollable elements—scratches on the film, slight movement in the camera, and slight signs of breathing and occasional blinks by Cunningham—become the work's animation. And perhaps most pronounced of all, the film's sound (basically silence, but with all the aggregations of hums, fuzz and drones this brings), in combination with the sound of the actual projectors whirring away, produced an awesome roar in the space, the sound of raw vitality, which, when Cunningham happened to pass away halfway through the exhibition, assumed an even more existentially charged character.

JS —— The other week I saw Tacita's *Merce Cunningham* installation for the first time myself, in Hannover. It's a revelation. The shock of stillness and the noise of silence… It's really a magisterial piece, and yet (almost) nothing happens. I felt excited and jealous… I still do!

All the projections have Cunningham in natural size, which invites the shadows of the audience into his space. This makes for an interactive element, but nevertheless the whole work is focused on a *compelling image* quite contrary to Fluxus ... (or at least my possibly ill-informed view of Fluxus).

I also saw the European première of her new film, *Craneway Event*, which Cunningham asked her to make after he saw that first project. It follows three days of his company rehearsing, watched by him, from a wheelchair. They are in an extraordinarily light-filled industrial hall by the sea, outside San Francisco. The film is very long, almost two hours, and thus makes quite a contrast to the installation. Just the idea of watching an art film (and about dance!) this long really made me cringe in advance ... but I sat through it and at the end I was happy to have done so. I had entered a space and hung out there, and at some point I realized I was living in such an amazing image. The film (the viewer?) needed this long stretch of time to become more than an image, to become a reality. Sadly, Merce Cunningham never saw this particular image made from his reality.

I have been thinking a lot about a comment you made in Venice when we compared notes on an underwhelming Biennale. You said something like: 'In the end, it's all about making compelling images'. Something we both sagely agreed was lacking in that particular setting.

But what does 'compelling' really mean in this context? Do you know?

TN —— 'Compelling' risks being a less dumb version of 'good', or another way to say 'I like that picture'. Perhaps it is attractive because it suggests a state of compulsion. To look at a great image is to feel some state of shock. Or perhaps a *process* of shock. 'Process' because the experience does not recede, but seems to flow on, even intensify as we spend time with the image. The sentence 'the image compels us' has the image as the subject of the sentence. And our own compulsions respond to and feed on the image. 'Compelling' expresses an interchange between me and what is before me—a difficult-to-pin-down motion between what is seen (outside me) and my being (or a flow of perceiving inside me)—that is also a slow exhilaration. I visited the Morandi Museum in Bologna late last year and I felt that interchange very strongly. Those paintings of ten or so unremarkable objects in all those rooms of the museum were deeply arresting. They represent something of the compulsions of Morandi. Very distant indeed from what we associate with a 'public address'. But those paintings seem to reach into every corner of our human experience, and they connect to our own compulsions, certain desires for meanings refracted in everyday objects, and in stillness.

It sounds facile, or simply a retreat into a kind of romanticism, but part of the appeal of a great image is that on the one hand we recognize it, it rings true with a certain familiarity, and on the other hand it is compelling because we don't know what we are looking at, we don't know why we are moved. I can only compare it to the sensation of laughing at a joke, but before we do the retrospective mental work to understand why the joke might be funny. Again, at the risk of lapsing into an easy romanticism, I think this unknownness is also part of the image's creation. Gerhard Richter made tens of thousands of small decisions to create each of his Baader-Meinhof paintings. They could not be further from acts of blind creation. But even in these decisions, with a set of paintings that are ostensibly replicating found photographs, the image is interesting because it has been discovered.

Richter's paintings return me to Fluxus. In one sense, the indeterminacy of Fluxus, the privileging of chance and the repudiation of the art object's authority, operates against the carefully orchestrated image. Fluxus is against that idea of the compelling image in the same way that it is against the monument, and the grand piano. Maciunas even wrote a family tree for Fluxus, with Byzantine Iconoclasm at the top, a very overt linking of the joyful cheekiness of Fluxus and an aggressive suspicion of images. But that indeterminacy which Fluxus holds dear is also *part of* the image's relationship to discovery. It is part of *opening up* the image to the unknown (in its creation), and part of what *opens out* as the unknown (in our apprehension of that image). Richter's processes of negation (his use of the squeegee, for example, in his non-figurative paintings) allow the indeterminate into the making of his images. These processes are also critical to the indeterminacy that is central to our experience of those paintings, their refusal of what we seek in them, of solidity, of grounding. I find it hard to leave Fluxus (and especially Cage) at the moment because of this fraught relation between the image and indeterminacy, a relation which oscillates between feeding and banishing, destroying and reinstating. The image needs its own dissembling into indeterminacy to maintain its connection to living, indeed to maintain its own life.

Perhaps this is a more complex answer to what I mean by 'compelling', something beyond my attempt in Venice to say 'I like it' in a less facile way! It is also part of what animates those Merce films by Tacita. The roar of all those whirring projectors and the stillness of Merce himself seem to have the image and the indeterminate very delicately posed in relation to one another, in suspense.

JS —— We started this dialogue in my hemisphere, in a cold Helsinki. Now I am heading in your direction, to Melbourne, and then onwards to the centre of Australia. I'm about to visit a place which 40 years ago was the birthplace, in a narrow sense, of some extraordinarily *compelling* images; ones which give Richter's a good run, if not yet for their money, then certainly for their content, any day. I am talking about the work of artists like Johnny Warrangkula Tjupurrula, Anatjari Tjampitjinpa, Shorty Lungkata Tjungurrayi, Mick Wallankarri Tjakamarra and several others. Artists who, like Richter, have made paintings I can't forget and that I find myself thinking about every so often.

I am writing in the plane which is soon to land in Melbourne. Right now we are passing above Adelaide, after having made our way in the skies above salt lakes and never-ending deserts. There's been a lot of travelling reflected in the way this, our dialogue, has developed over the past two years. You and I have journeyed both in a physical sense and in imagination. Lately you have been discussing Fluxus, a word which means 'to flow'. I understand the ethos of that art movement [*sic!*] as prescribing that images must be in motion (which can have more than one meaning) in order to retain value. Images in movement is what your banner marches propose: hand painted faces hoisted high and carried through the city. Painted images that describe movement and record travel is also what the artists I just mentioned produced: 'travel lines'.

It might seem I'm now into celebrating travel... One may get the impression we've come a long way from the solidity of my chimneys (though the associations they make are fluid) and my analogy of the impregnable fortress city watched from the outside. Yet this image of sealed-up stillness is, don't forget, visited and viewed by a passing traveller, who temporarily halts to gaze at its mysterious construction... He or she would certainly have circled it to see if there was any secret opening before eventually deciding to continue, the memory of a compelling sight lodged at a secret location somewhere in the brain.

TN —— It is the stillness in Cage's *4'33"* that allows the flux of everyday sounds to enter —*and be*—the piece. Stillness generates its indeterminacy.

Stillness is not always like this. Part of what fails about the classical nineteenth-century monuments that litter our cities is their monumental stillness, which becomes a kind of invisibility to the life that swarms around them. If they are redeemed in any way it is through the inadvertent meanings that this life around them provides. Last week, the monument to Redmond Barry (a famous colonial judge) outside the State

Library, momentarily seemed interesting, as it presided over a conflict between two small demonstrations, a pro-Palestinian group of students and a Zionist counter-demonstration.

It is interesting that we have almost exclusively talked about still images in this conversation. That still images arrest movements, and in turn generate them, becoming animate or animating *us*, through our encounter with them, is a large part of what I enjoy about them. It's also part of my recurrent interest in still images of flags in 92
motion, that endless motion caused by the movement of the air, with its connection to our own breathing, the movement which keeps us living.

We stood together in front of some of those great Papunya paintings yesterday at the National Gallery here in Melbourne. They are self-evidently still—like Richter's squeegee paintings—but part of their force is their suggestion of movement. Of course the 'etymology' of those pictures is in paintings which were not 'pulled out of time', like a painting in a museum. They were ephemeral, and, when painted onto the body, they were literally animated. There is some important 'after-image' of those movements of the body in the paintings we looked at yesterday, like the extraordinary visual pulse in that Yala Yala Gibbs Tjungurrayi *Snake and Water Dreaming* painting. As much as the suggestion of cartography or mapping of movement through a landscape, this echo of the body's movement is part of what I think these paintings animate *in us*, and is central to their inventiveness as works of contemporary art, as acts of translation.

I am reminded of the drawings of the nineteenth-century Wurundjeri political
86 leader and artist, William Barak, whose drawings I hoped we might find upstairs in the National Gallery yesterday. Barak worked (at the same time as Redmond Barry) at the Aboriginal mission station, Coranderrk, near present-day Healesville.[6] His drawings of Wurundjeri ceremonies and historical events give form to memories, not just seen but heard and felt. The movement of the figures who dance and sing in his pictures themselves enact memories, so that drawing and dancing reciprocate. The pictorial liveliness of Barak's drawings—the way the rhythms of human movement are so beautifully evoked by the patterning of the pictorial space—is in part this reciprocation, this interchange between drawing and dancing as ways to remember, as ways to enact the past into the present.

88 **JS** —— I'm on the way back from Papunya. We drove there on red desert roads, on which anything could happen. Without warning

there were wild camels right in front of us. The wide road would suddenly narrow, or it would become so corrugated that the 4WD shook like a spaceship at takeoff. Every once in a while we crossed a tiny river bed (with water flowing—the Centre has seen a lot of rain in recent weeks) or careened through giant puddles as wide as the road itself, throwing huge wedges of red liquid to either side.

There were five of us in that sturdy car. Two friends from Melbourne, two from Alice Springs, and then me: a Swede from Berlin, who had caused the trip to happen through my obsessive desire to see the place where the 'Painting Movement' got started in 1971, when Aboriginal people of mixed tribal affiliation set about creating, on board and canvas, acrylic paintings of a type never before seen. Crucially, these paintings were made to address 'the Other' (that is, us), and they aimed to communicate in a visual language both old and new ideas and narratives. It certainly was a very particular form of public address and the initiative would eventually lead to change and development in many areas, in a way which must have astonished the originators of this address.

Over the years, the visual language used here has continually developed, and a huge industry of both commerce and interpretation has grown up around it. Painters have

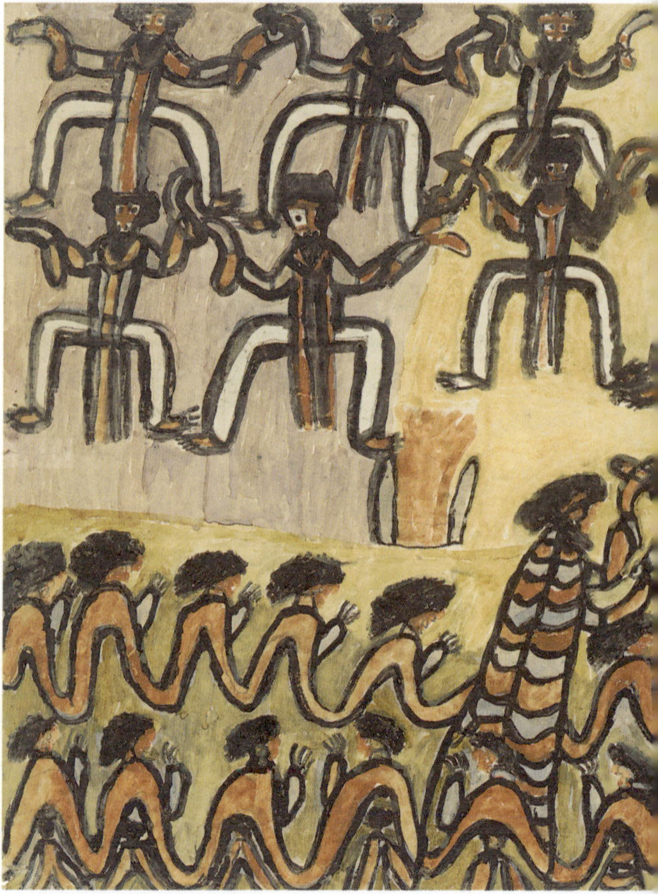

William Barak
Wurundjeri c.1824–1903
Ceremony, late 1890s
pencil, wash, ground wash, charcoal, gouache and earth pigments
57.0 × 88.8 cm
National Gallery of Victoria, Melbourne
Purchased 1962

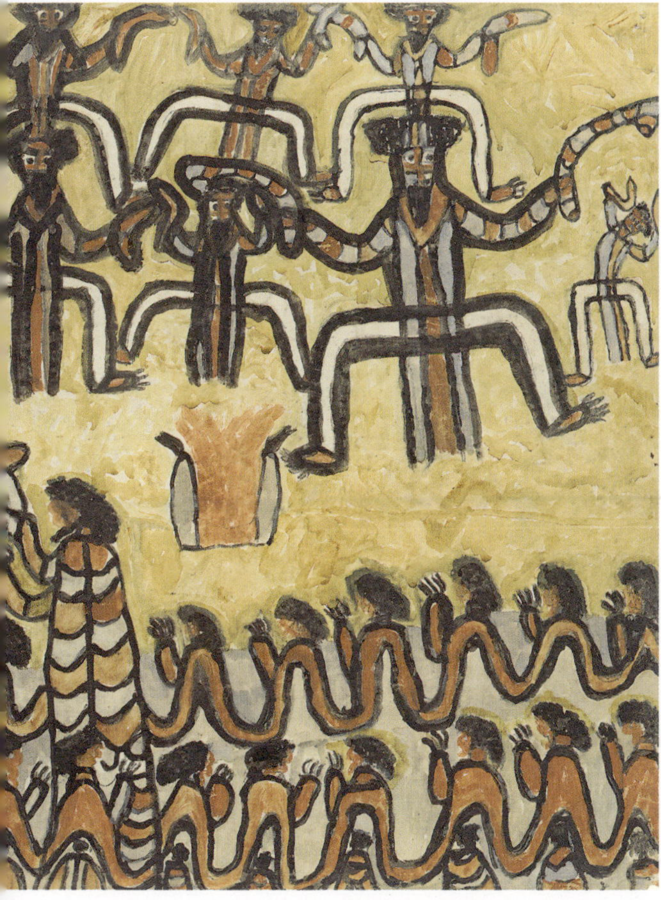

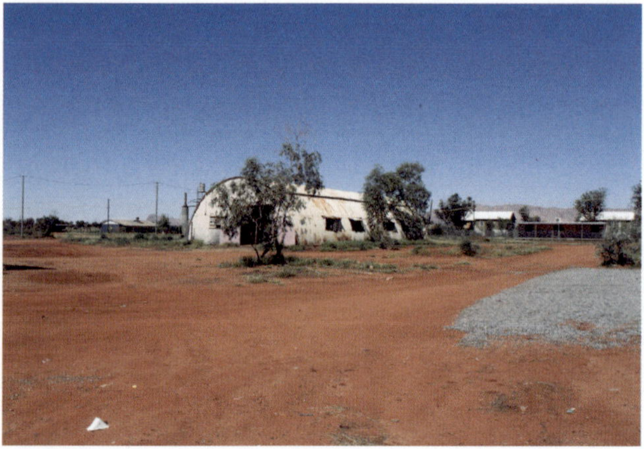

Papunya, Northern Territory, 17 April 2010. Photograph: Jan Svenungsson.

become public names, exhibitions have travelled the world, money and prestige has been in circulation. I, personally, have looked at images made here which, put simply, inspire deep emotion and intellectual excitement in me. Meanwhile, many Aboriginal people continue to live in misery, and reconciliation between the cultures—one based on equality—is very hard to foresee.

Papunya is not exactly a tourist magnet, but I have known for years that one day I would have to see it. On the way to fulfilling this perhaps irrational desire, I have learnt many things.

We arrived shortly before midday. It was hot. Very still. A small number of buildings scattered lazily in the endless expanse of red sand. Some in bad shape, trash on the ground; others well kept. The famous school,[7] expanded with new pavilions, was enclosed by a fence, gates locked. It was Saturday and no-one was about. It was hot, very hot. It was still.

How can something so important have ever happened in such a remote and arid place?

But it did.

I walked around, taking photographs of places and buildings and emptiness. I compared reality to a painting I made three years ago, after I'd discovered through satellite photos that the layout of this community is

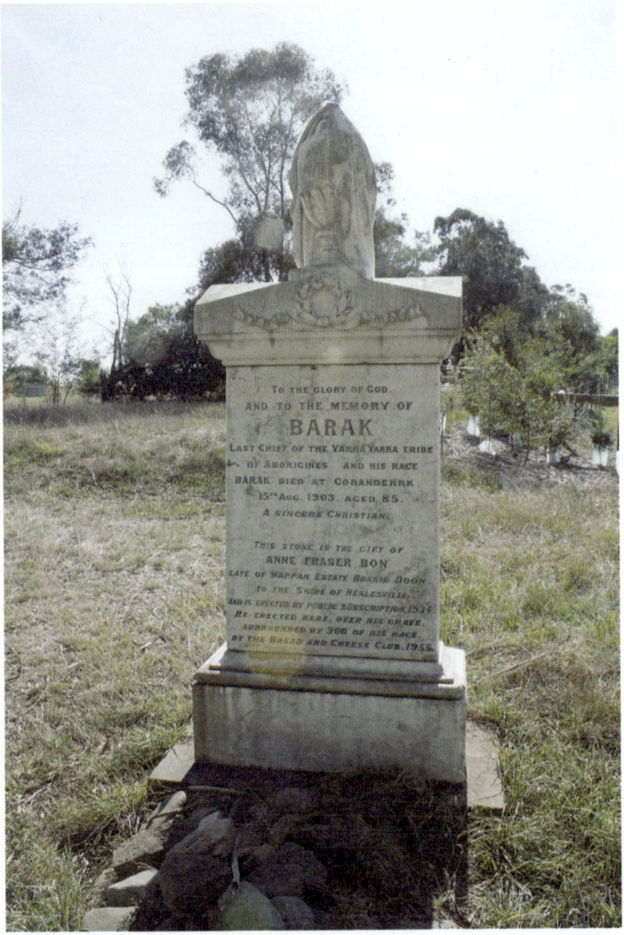

Barak's gravestone, Coranderrk cemetery, Victoria, 20 April 2010.
Photograph: Jan Svenungsson.

itself like a painting, a traditional 'honey ant' design. On the ground I couldn't see it: I was too close to the brushstrokes—or pixels.

People live and work there, but to me it remained a fortress, a place I could only really watch from the outside, even while being very close. What really takes place inside, I must imagine.

Nevertheless, it was deeply emotional to walk in the hot red sand between the disused painting hall of rusty corrugated iron and the well-kept school in Papunya.

I felt happy.

TN —— The day after you returned to Melbourne from Alice, we drove to Coranderrk, through the lush hills around Healesville, the area to the north-east of Melbourne through which those cataclysmic bushfires raged last year. I wondered then if you were thinking about your drive from Alice to Papunya from a few days earlier. There were no corrugated roads on our trip, no red sand, not even much left of the old mission station we had gone to see. Though Coranderrk is only an hour from Melbourne, I have studied images from and of that place for several years without managing to go there, mostly looking at, admiring, trying to understand, the watercolours which Barak made there. What we did see, the remnants of the Coranderrk cemetery, was deeply

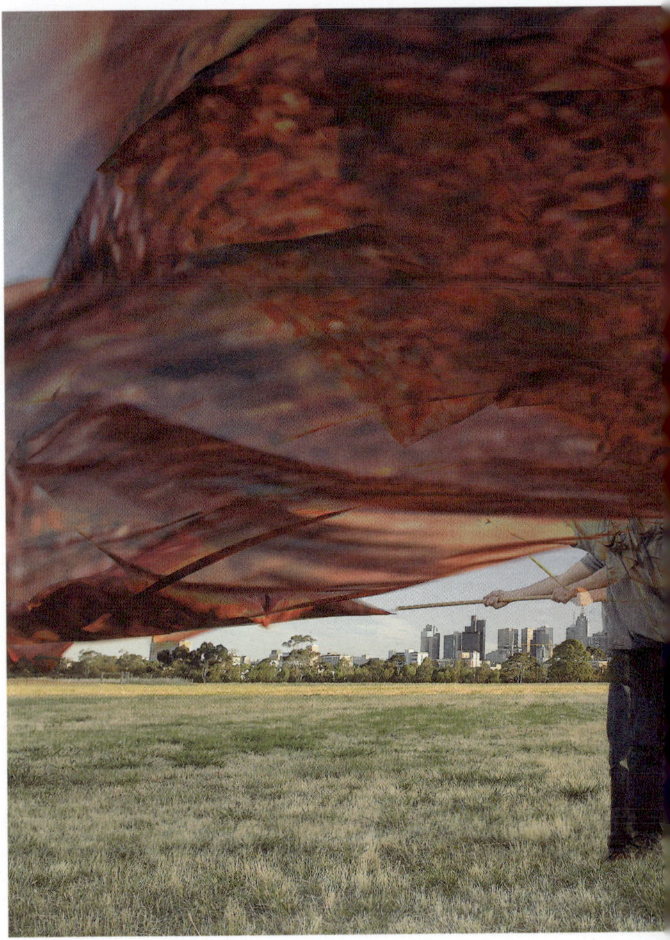

Tom Nicholson, *Nardoo flagwave*, 2009–10. Type C photograph, 150 × 100 cm.
Imaging: Christian Capurro.

Nardoo flagwave is an off-shoot of *Monument for the flooding of Royal Park*, a video and artist's book which draws on the deaths of the Australian explorers Burke and Wills, caused by eating Nardoo sporocarps at Coopers Creek in 1861. The Yantruwanta people of the region around Coopers Creek prepared these sporocarps as a flour in a way that neutralized the Nardoo's thiaminase, but their offers of hospitality to the two explorers were violently rejected by Burke, who was deeply hostile towards Aboriginal people and

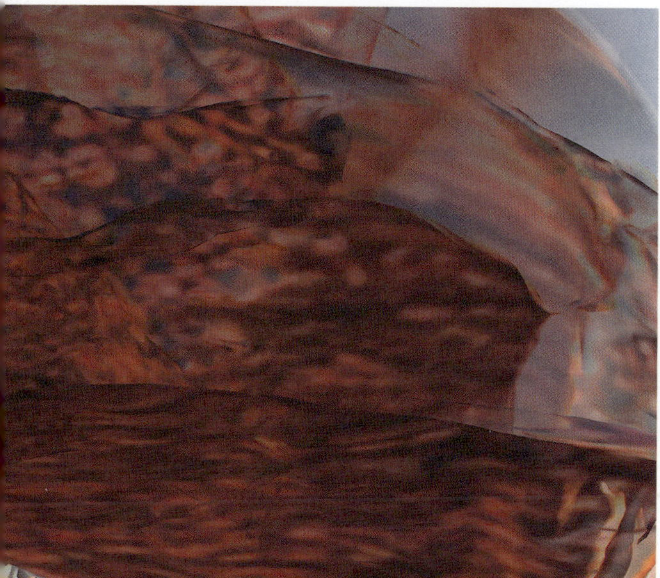

the idea of any dependence upon them. Attempting to emulate the use of the sporocarps, Burke and Wills spent their final days gorging on a plant that disabled their digestive systems. The Nardoo plant is also remarkable for its prolific growth after desert floods. As the floodwaters recede, Nardoo dries into vast expanses of red, which Nicholson's work proposes as an alternative monument at the site of Burke and Wills' departure, Royal Park, in Melbourne's inner north.

moving. Not only the modest monument to Barak erected after his death, but also the list of names of the people who are known to be buried there, assembled on one plaque, mounted on a cairn in the middle of the old cemetery. The cemetery's small collection of cairns, plaques, a handful of gravestones, the monument to Barak, jumbled together in a small space surrounded by farmland, no-one else in sight, was hardly overwhelming in itself. To wander between this jumble became affecting because these things were charged by images: the drawings of Barak, and the archival photographs of Coranderrk that survive from the 19th century. The public forms of commemoration in the cemetery become powerful through an imaginary presence. It is this presence—the memory of looking at those Barak drawings of singing and dancing, held within us as we walk among that motley set of monuments—which animate their address and which in turn animate something in us. Their address becomes living. We feel *our* living. Something still roars.

NOTES

1 Ramones, 'Today Your Love, Tomorrow the World', on *Ramones* (Sire Records, 1976).

2 Many above-ground air raid shelters built in Nazi Germany sported balcony-like ornaments to suggest that the Führer might appear at any moment and deliver a rousing speech.

3 'The silence of Marcel Duchamp is overrated.'

4 'The babbling of Beuys likewise.'

5 I know we could have a long discussion on 'how do you know it is art', but that goes beyond my point here. The designation of the figurine as art was not made by me.

6 Coranderrk was a mission station on the upper reaches of the Yarra River near present-day Healesville, about 50 kilometres north-east of Melbourne. Coranderrk was granted to the Wurundjeri (and other Aboriginal people from different language groups) after a long and extensive process of lobbying by Aboriginal leaders and European sympathizers, such as the Presbyterian lay preacher John Green. Much of the political activism which emanated from Coranderrk, led by such figures as Simon Wonga and William Barak, centred on Coranderrk and the defence of its autonomy. Critical to this activism was contending with the 1886 'Half-Caste Act', formally known as Aborigines Protection Act. The communities at Coranderrk and other missions such as Lake Condah were active in contesting the Act, albeit unsuccessfully. The life of the community at Coranderrk is represented in a remarkable body of late-nineteenth-century photography, a medium which the Wurundjeri consciously adopted to press their claims for self-determination. The mission was formally closed in 1924 and most residents were forced to move to Lake Tyers Mission. Five older people refused to move and continued living at Coranderrk until their deaths.

7 On the wall of which, in 1971, the newly arrived teacher, Geoffrey Bardon, invited a group of men to create a mural painting. This became the seminal event that launched the Painting Movement. This Honey Ant Dreaming mural was painted over by the white authorities in 1974, a most unfortunate act.

Forms for a public address was written in the form of a correspondence between 16 February 2008 and 1 June 2010.

The authors would like to thank the many individuals and institutions who supported the reproduction of various images: The People's History Museum, Manchester, UK, particularly Phil Dunn; the National Gallery of Victoria, particularly Judith Ryan and Jennie Moloney; Viscopy; Fred Torres; Tacita Dean; Călin Dan and Josif Kiraly; the Herald and Weekly Times; the University of Tübingen.

We thank Roger Averill for his editing work on this text.

Forms for a Public Address was generously supported by a Publication Grant from the Faculty of Art & Design, Monash University, and we are grateful for this generosity, and for the support of Dr Anne Marsh, Kathie Barwick, Dr Paul Jones and Kit Wise.

Finally, we are grateful to Brad Haylock, whose dedication and skill has given this exchange its own public form.

Tom Nicholson is an artist who lives in Melbourne. He is represented by Anna Schwartz Gallery, Melbourne, and is a Lecturer in Drawing at the Faculty of Art & Design, Monash University. — www.tomn.net

Jan Svenungsson is a Swedish artist based in Berlin. He is represented by Galerie Werner Klein, Cologne and Galleri Flach, Stockholm. — www.jansvenungsson.com

Brad Haylock is an artist and designer who lives and works in Melbourne. He is a Lecturer in Visual Communication at Monash University. — www. bradhaylock.com

---

Forms for a public address
Tom Nicholson and Jan Svenungsson

Editor: Roger Averill

First edition 2011
ISBN: 978-0-9807536-6-0

Published by Surpllus Pty Ltd, Melbourne, Australia.
Printed by BPA Print Group, on Impact paper.
Typeset in Freya and Monotype Grotesque families.

Surpllus Pty Ltd
PO Box 418
Flinders Lane 8009
Victoria, Australia
www.surpllus.com

Surpllus #6